LEON.

HAPPY SALADS

BY JANE BAXTER & JOHN VINCENT

FROM FARMS
WE TRUST

CONTENTS

INTRODUCTION

We have loved writing this book. It has made us very happy. We started Leon to make it easy for everyone to eat well – by providing naturally fast food, and also by sharing our recipes and ideas in books like this.

THERE ARE FIVE 'PRINCIPLES' BEHIND LEON:

1.
THE FOOD MUST TASTE FANTASTIC.

2.
IT MUST BE REMARKABLY GOOD FOR YOU.

3.
YOU MUST FEEL GOOD AFTER YOU EAT IT.

4.
IT HAS TO BE KIND TO THE PLANET.

5.
IT HAS TO BE AFFORDABLE.

Salads are one of the most powerful ways of achieving these things. We see it as one of our principal tasks to make vegetables taste good.

The recipes in this book have been designed to be good for you and good for the planet. Our bodies have needs (not those), and the big body called Earth we live on has needs, some of which we are dangerously ignoring. Veg goes a long way to sorting them both out.

IT'S CLEAR THAT VEGETABLES, AS WELL AS THE CHILDREN, ARE OUR FUTURE.

Vegetables provide us with natural energy, with the fibre, antioxidants and other nutrients that we need and they help us to keep our gut well, and to heal it. And the olive oil you drizzle on to your salad, for almost all metabolic types, is giving you the good fat you need to function and flourish.

Why 'Happy Salads'? Happy because these salads just look happy. Happy because they signify happy occasions. Happy because you will love eating them. Happy because you will feel good afterwards. Happy because if you make them a big part of your diet, you will feel well and energized. They put us in a good mood, and we think they will do the same for you.

We have set out to create your Desert Island Discs salad book. The only salad book you will ever need to own. Every recipe you will find here is a main meal in itself. Classics. Leon classics. And a lot of brand spankingly new ones.

THE BOOK

WE HAVE DIVIDED THE BOOK INTO 5 SECTIONS.

1. CLASSICS: These are the salads that you know and love and have always wanted to make. They may not be strict classics, we've given some of them a little Leon twist, but they'll certainly make you nostalgic, and very, very hungry.

2. NATURALLY FAST: The salads in this section all take 20 minutes or fewer to prepare. Make them in a hurry, or take your time, they will taste fantastic and satisfy you.

3. LUNCHBOX: The recipes in this section are to serve one person. They're designed for you time. It's your lunch hour, and it's time you took it back. The salads chosen here will all hold well if prepared the night before and dressed just before eating.

4. FOOD FOR FRIENDS: These recipes are ones we think of as dinner party dishes. The stand-out salads. The 'how on earth did you make this taste so good' salads. The secret is, they're really not very hard to make, they just require a few more specialist ingredients.

5. FOOD FOR FAMILY: These are family suppers, Sunday roasts and holiday picnic salads. Big, crowd-pleasing salads.

KEY				
WF	**GF**	**DF**	**V**	**VE**
WHEAT FREE	GLUTEN FREE	DAIRY FREE	VEGETARIAN	VEGAN

HOW TO MAKE THE BEST SALAD YOU'VE EVER HAD: TASTE, TEXTURE & ARCHITECTURE

The spectrum of ingredients that can be used, and the huge array of ways they can be served – hot, cold, in a jar or on a stick – makes salads ideal for experimentation and creativity. The first salad that popped up after a quick search on Pinterest was, 'Snickers Caramel Apple Salad', so a salad really is what you make of it. Here are the three points that we think you should have in the back of your mind when constructing yours.

TASTE: A good balance of flavours is important when cooking anything, especially when putting together a good salad. Salty, sweet, acidic and bitter flavours should all be in harmony. It's important to taste your dressing and ingredients as you go. Your instinct will tell you what's right and whether you should season more.

TEXTURE: It's crucial to look at the salad as a whole. Try to get a range of textures in there – from crunchy, to chewy, to smooth.

ARCHITECTURE: If you are combining a variety of cooked vegetables in your salad, try to vary the cooking techniques. Try combining a mixture of grilling, roasting, steaming and raw vegetables. Also think about how the salad will look – we all eat with our eyes – and if cutting different vegetables certain ways will enhance the overall appearance.

> **THESE ARE THE ONLY SALAD RECIPES YOU NEED TO KNOW. THEY ARE FOR PEOPLE WHO ALREADY LOVE SALADS, AND FOR PEOPLE WHO DON'T KNOW IT YET.**

SALAD STORECUPBOARD

A storecupboard list to use in (safely) sexing up any basic salad.

VINEGARS

RED WINE
BALSAMIC
BASIC WHITE WINE
SPECIALITY TYPES
LIKE CHAMPAGNE & MOSCATEL
RICE WINE
CIDER
SHERRY

OILS

OLIVE: LIGHT & GOOD-QUALITY
EXTRA VIRGIN
WALNUT
RAPESEED
SUNFLOWER
GRAPESEED
COCONUT
SESAME

SPECIALITY ASIAN

MIRIN
TAMARIND PASTE
DRIED SHRIMPS
WASABI PASTE
FISH SAUCE
KECAP MANIS
COCONUT MILK
WAKAME/DRIED SEAWEED
PALM SUGAR
TAMARI/SOY
DESICCATED COCONUT
SHRIMP PASTE/BLACHAN
IKAN BILIS

NUTS & SEEDS

WALNUTS
ALMONDS & SMOKED ALMONDS
HAZELNUTS
PEANUTS
PISTACHIOS
PUMPKIN SEEDS
GOLDEN LINSEEDS
SUNFLOWER SEEDS
SESAME SEEDS: BLACK & WHITE

SWEET THINGS

RAISINS
DRIED APRICOTS
DRIED CRANBERRIES
DRIED PEARS
DRIED FIGS
SOFT BROWN SUGAR
RUNNY HONEY
MAPLE SYRUP
DATE SYRUP
POMEGRANATE MOLASSES

GRAINS

BLACK RICE
BROWN JASMINE RICE
LONG-GRAIN RICE
FARRO
FREGOLA
BULGUR
QUINOA
ORZO
DITALINI
RICE NOODLES
BLACK RICE NOODLES/SOBA
POLENTA
ISRAELI COUSCOUS/MAFTOUL
FREEKAH

PULSES

BLACK BEANS
BORLOTTI BEANS
HARICOT BEANS
CANNELLINI BEANS
PUY OR CASTELLUCIO LENTILS

FROZEN

PEAS
BROAD BEANS
EDAMAME BEANS
SWEETCORN

SPICES

CAYENNE PEPPER

SUMAC

FENNEL SEEDS

ALLSPICE

NUTMEG

CINNAMON

DRIED OREGANO

SAFFRON

GROUND CUMIN & SEEDS

GROUND CORIANDER & SEEDS

SMOKED & SWEET PAPRIKA

OTHER

TINNED TUNA

SALTED CAPERS

ANCHOVIES

MUSTARDS: DIJON, WHOLE
& ENGLISH

ENGLISH MUSTARD POWDER

HORSERADISH CREAM

WORCESTERSHIRE SAUCE

TOMATO KETCHUP

TABASCO/CHILLI SAUCE

GHERKINS

CHIPOTLE SAUCE

PIQUILLO PEPPERS

BLACK/GREEN OLIVES

CORN TORTILLAS

PREPPY PREPPING

WASHING AND DRYING LETTUCE – No matter how much 'ready-washed' salad you buy, it's always worth an extra rinse. When using smaller greens, wash them carefully in a sink of cold water. Turn them over and lift them out into a colander. Dry them in batches (don't cram them in or the leaves will bruise), using a salad spinner. Remember, if the leaves are wet, the dressing won't cling to them.

HAVE THE RIGHT TOOLS – Every builder needs a sturdy toolkit, and as a salad architect, you'll want the best kit too. A (really) sharp knife, a good vegetable peeler, a pestle and mortar and a steamer are key. From there, getting your hands on a spiralizer, a food processor or stick blender and a mandolin will help to make salads swifter than ever.

PLATING/BOWLING – Rub your salad bowl with a clove of garlic and some olive oil and season it well before putting in your lettuce leaves to be dressed. This really makes a huge difference to the quality of the salad.

TOSSING – Use your hands – humans are a lot more delicate than salad spoons, and you'll be able to feel any dry patches that have missed a spot of dressing. It's best not to use your hands to serve though.

A NOTE ON DRESSINGS

We have given quantities for the dressings in this book, but it's a good idea to add a dressing gradually and see how much you need. When using delicate leaves like lamb's lettuce, frisée and rocket, dress the salad at the last minute and use the dressing sparingly. More robust greens like kale and cabbage won't suffer if they're dressed earlier. When dressing roasted root vegetables and other cooked ingredients, you'll get a better final result if you tip the cooked vegetables into the dressing while it's still hot.

CLASSICS

NIÇOISE

SERVES 2
PREP TIME: 15 MINS · COOK TIME: 15 MINS
WF · GF · DF

100g (3½oz) **new potatoes**, boiled and halved

150g (5½oz) **French beans**, cooked

2 **boiled eggs**, cut into wedges

6 **cherry tomatoes**, halved

¼ **cucumber**, peeled, chopped and deseeded

1 **shallot**, sliced

50g (1¾oz) **tinned tuna**, flaked

10 **black olives**, preferably **Niçoise**

2 **radishes**, sliced

a few **fresh basil leaves**, to serve

salt and **freshly ground black pepper**

DRESSING:

juice of 2 **tomatoes**, sieved

3 tablespoons **olive oil**

1 tablespoon **red wine vinegar**

1 teaspoon **capers**

2 **anchovies**

½ clove of **garlic**, crushed

4 **fresh basil leaves**

A nice classic from Nice.

Make the dressing by blitzing all the ingredients together in a food processor or with a stick blender. If neither is available, you can use a pestle and mortar. Season well.

Toss the potatoes and French beans with half of the dressing in a large bowl. Season, then gently fold through the rest of the ingredients and arrange on a serving plate. Drizzle with the rest of the dressing and sprinkle with roughly chopped basil leaves.

TIP
We find the perfect time for 2 medium boiled eggs is 6–7 minutes.

LYONNAISE

100g (3½oz) **bacon** or **pancetta lardons**
1 tablespoon **olive oil**
1 tablespoon **red wine vinegar**
1 **shallot**, finely chopped
1 teaspoon **Dijon mustard**
2 tablespoons **extra virgin olive oil**
a splash of **vinegar (white wine** or **malt)**
2 **eggs**
100g (3½oz) **frisée** or **curly endive**
croutons (optional, see page 214)

This salad is originally from Lyon, not Leon. Things change.

Cook the lardons in a frying pan with the olive oil for a few minutes until lightly browned and crisp. Remove with a slotted spoon on to some kitchen paper. Add the vinegar to the pan and scrape with a wooden spoon, followed by the shallot and mustard. Stir well and remove from the heat. Whisk in the extra virgin olive oil to finish the dressing.

Bring a pan of water with the vinegar up to a simmer. Crack the eggs into the water and poach gently for about 3 minutes, or until the whites have set. Remove from the pan with a slotted spoon on to kitchen paper to drain. Alternatively, you can soft-boil and peel the eggs.

Toss the frisée in the dressing and bacon lardons so that it's well coated. Divide between 2 plates and top each one with a poached egg.

Add croutons if you want to a bit more crunch, and if you don't need it to be gluten or wheat free.

\\\\ TIP ////

To poach eggs, crack them into small ramekins and slowly lower into simmering water that has been whisked vigorously.

PRAWN COCKTAIL HOUR

. . . .

SERVES 2
PREP TIME: 15 MINS
WF · GF · DF (only **GF** if no Worcestershire sauce)

. . . .

3–4 **watercress sprigs**

1 **little gem lettuce**, shredded

½ a large **avocado**, diced

¼ of a **cucumber**, peeled and diced

4 **spring onions**, chopped

2 tablespoons **lemon juice**

1 dessertspoon chopped **fresh chives**
    and **dill**

150–200g (5½–7oz) **cooked king prawns**,
    peeled

1 **radish**, thinly sliced and cut into
    fine needles

salt and **cayenne pepper**

DRESSING:

2 tablespoons **full-fat mayonnaise**

1 teaspoon **tomato ketchup**

a few drops of **chilli sauce** or **Tabasco**

a capful of **brandy**

horseradish or **Worcestershire sauce**,
    to taste (optional)

salt and **freshly ground black pepper**

This and disco defined the 1970s. Ideal for family get-togethers (nans love it) or any 70s-themed dinner party.

. . . .

On each plate start layering up the ingredients. First watercress, then the little gem, avocado, cucumber and spring onions. Sprinkle with lemon juice and half your herbs, then season with the salt and cayenne pepper.

Top the salad with the prawns and season again with salt and cayenne pepper.

Stir the dressing ingredients together and drizzle over the salad and prawns. Finish with the rest of the herbs and the radish needles.

\ \ \ \ **TIP** / / / /
You can add horseradish or Worcestershire sauce to taste. Jane likes punchy flavours, so she uses both to give it a bit more oomph.

THE ORIGINAL SUPERFOOD SALAD

SERVES 2
PREP TIME: 10 MINS · COOK TIME: 5 MINS
WF · GF · V

⅔ of a head of **broccoli**, cut into bite-size
    florets, stalks peeled and sliced
120g (4¼oz) **frozen peas**, defrosted
¼ of a **cucumber**, cut into slim batons
100g (3½oz) good-quality **feta**, crumbled
2 tablespoons **Leon toasted seeds** (see
    page 215)
½ an **avocado**, cut into pieces
100g (3½oz) **cooked quinoa**, cooled
a small handful of **fresh flat-leaf parsley**,
    roughly chopped
a small handful of **fresh mint**,
    roughly chopped
3 tablespoons **French vinaigrette**
    (see page 216)

This bowl of goodness has been on our menu since we opened our doors in 2004. It truly is the original – when we googled it before launching, it didn't exist. Over the years, we've changed and grown a lot, but Leon evangelists will never let this one go.

Put 2cm/¾ inch of hot water into a saucepan with a pinch of salt and cover the pan. Once boiling, drop in the broccoli and put the lid back on. Drain after 3 minutes, then run the broccoli under cold water to take all the heat out and keep it good and green.

Now build your salad in layers: broccoli, peas, cucumber, feta, avocado, quinoa and finally the herbs and seeds. Dress the salad just before you eat it.

\\\ TIP ///
We no longer use alfalfa sprouts, but they're a lovely topper if you have any.

FATTOUSH

SERVES 2

PREP TIME: 15 MINS · COOK TIME: 5 MINS

DF · V · Ve

1 small **pitta bread**

2 tablespoons **olive oil**

a pinch of **sumac**

1 **Little Gem lettuce**, chopped

½ **cucumber**, deseeded, roughly peeled
    and diced into 1–2cm (½–¾ inch) cubes

2 **plum tomatoes**, cored and diced

4 **spring onions**, chopped

2 **radishes,** chopped

1 tablespoon chopped **fresh
    flat-leaf parsley**

1 tablespoon chopped **fresh mint**

salt and **freshly ground black pepper**

DRESSING:

2 tablespoons **lemon juice**

3 tablespoons **olive oil**

a pinch of **sumac**

a pinch of **allspice**

a pinch of **ground cinnamon**

salt and **freshly ground black pepper**

This Middle Eastern bread salad is full of colour, freshness and a little crunch, and was a big favourite of John's when he lived near the Edgware Road. Unlikely to make you fat, no matter what the name might suggest.

Toast the pitta in a toaster until just browned. Heat the oil in a small frying pan, then cut the pitta into roughly 2cm (¾ inch) pieces, dust with sumac and fry in the oil, turning to coat for 2–3 minutes or until crisp.

Mix all the rest of the salad ingredients together in a large bowl and season well.

Whisk together the dressing ingredients and season.

Just before serving, toss the salad with the dressing and fold in the pitta pieces.

＼＼＼ TIP ／／／
Other veg can be used in this salad – try blanched broad beans and shaved fennel, with a touch of toasted cumin in the dressing.

GREEK

SERVES 2
PREP TIME: 20 MINS · COOK TIME: 5 MINS
V (check feta for vegetarian status)

½ **cucumber**, peeled and sliced

½ **red onion**, sliced

6 **cherry tomatoes**, halved

½ **green pepper**, deseeded and sliced

1 tablespoon chopped **fresh flat-leaf parsley**

12 **black olives**

100g (3½oz) **feta**

2 tablespoons **plain flour**

1 **egg**, beaten

2 tablespoons **panko breadcrumbs**

3 tablespoons **olive oil**

DRESSING:

3 tablespoons **olive oil**

1 tablespoon **red wine vinegar**

1 clove of **garlic**, crushed

a pinch of **dried oregano**

In this recipe we've fried the feta for a change. The combination of warm soft cheese with the crisp salad is worthy of a Homerian epic, but it is different from the classic Greek salad. If you prefer a more traditional dish, just slice the cheese on top of the dressed salad. Dedicated to Yiannis, John's friend in Meganisi.

Whisk together all the dressing ingredients.

Prepare the vegetables and set to one side.

Cut the feta into two pieces. Dip them first in the flour, then in the beaten egg and finally in the breadcrumbs. Fry for a couple of minutes in the hot oil over a medium heat until the coating is well browned, then remove the feta from the pan and leave to drain on kitchen paper.

Dress the salad and arrange on a serving plate. Top with the fried cheese.

> **\\\\ TIP ////**
> You can top the salad with roasted halloumi crumbs (see page 215) instead of feta.

TABBOULEH

SERVES 2
PREP TIME: 20 MINS (plus soaking)
DF · V · Ve

50g (1¾oz) **bulgur wheat**

50g (1¾oz) **fresh flat-leaf parsley**, chopped

20g (¾oz) **fresh mint**, chopped

100g (3½oz) **tomatoes**, cored and diced

6 **spring onions**, chopped

2 tablespoons **lemon juice**

3 tablespoons **olive oil**

a pinch of **allspice**

a pinch of **sumac**

salt and **freshly ground black pepper**

In Lebanon, where this salad originates, National Tabbouleh Day is celebrated every year on the first Saturday of July. It's one of the most popular dishes in the Middle East, and in both our households too.

Put the bulgur wheat into a bowl and pour over 100ml (3½fl oz) of boiling water. Cover tightly with clingfilm, leave for 30 minutes (or until fluffed up), then uncover and leave to cool.

Place the soaked bulgur in a large bowl and add all the other ingredients. Mix well and season.

TIP

John makes his with quinoa when he doesn't fancy gluten.

WALDORF

50g (1¾oz) **walnut pieces**
a large pinch of **cayenne pepper**
1 teaspoon **olive oil**
2 **celery sticks**, cut lengthways and diced
1 large **red apple**, diced
20 **seedless grapes**, halved
4 **spring onions**, chopped
1 tablespoon chopped **fresh chives**
1 tablespoon chopped **fresh tarragon**
1 tablespoon **full-fat mayonnaise**
2 tablespoons **lemon juice**
leaves from 1 **Little Gem lettuce**
salt and **freshly ground black pepper**

Contrary to what you might believe from watching that **Fawlty Towers** *episode, the ingredients for this are very easy to source, put together and serve. You don't have to be in a fancy hotel in NYC to enjoy the Waldorf. But we guess it helps.*

Heat the oven to 150°C/300°F/Gas Mark 2.

Place the walnut pieces on a baking tray and sprinkle with cayenne pepper, olive oil and salt to taste. Massage this into the nuts and bake in the oven for 10 minutes, then leave to cool.

Cut all the fruit and vegetables into roughly the same size pieces. Toss them in a large bowl with the chopped herbs, mayonnaise and cooled walnuts. Season well with salt and pepper.

Spoon the salad on to the Little Gem leaves and serve.

\\\\ TIP ////

This salad could be dressed with a lighter herby dressing, or yoghurt could be used instead of mayonnaise if you don't need it to be dairy free.

SOM TAM

SERVES 2
PREP TIME: 20 MINS
WF · GF · DF

1 clove of **garlic**

2 small **Thai red chillies**, chopped

1 tablespoon **dried shrimps**

1 tablespoon **palm sugar** or **soft brown sugar**

juice of 1 **lime**

1 tablespoon **fish sauce**

½ a **green papaya** or **unripe mango**, peeled and shredded (or grated)

1 **carrot**, peeled and grated

3 **cherry tomatoes**, quartered

50g (1¾oz) **French beans**, cut into 2cm (¾ inch) lengths

2 tablespoons roasted **peanuts**, chopped

¼ of an **iceberg lettuce**, chopped

This recipe uses unripe papaya, but if this is unavailable try unripe mango or a combination of finely shredded white cabbage and mooli. The 'unripeness' of the fruit brings both fragrance and texture. You should definitely make it Som Tam.

In a pestle and mortar, grind together the garlic with the chillies and dried shrimps until you have a paste.

Add the sugar, lime juice and fish sauce and mix well. The secret to this dressing is having a good balance between these three ingredients. Keep tasting the mixture as you do it, adding more of each as you like.

In a large bowl, toss this dressing with all the remaining ingredients except the iceberg lettuce.

Arrange the lettuce on a serving plate and top with the dressed ingredients.

ROCKET MELON

SERVES 2
PREP TIME: 5 MINS
WF · GF · DF

½ a **canteloupe melon**
4–6 slices of **prosciutto**
a handful of **rocket**
olive oil
raw baby peas or **broad beans** (optional)

This is the perfect blend of salty, peppery and fresh(y).

Peel the melon and shave the flesh into thin strips with a vegetable peeler. Rip the prosciutto into strips and arrange on a serving plate with the melon, gently folding through the rocket.

Serve drizzled with olive oil, and scattered with peas or beans if you're using them.

\\\\ TIP ////
For a more traditional dish, serve the melon in wedges.

RUSSIAN

100g (3½oz) **fresh** or **frozen peas**

100g (3½oz) **carrots**, peeled

150g (5½oz) **waxy potatoes**, peeled

½ a **red onion**, finely chopped

1 tablespoon **red wine vinegar**

1 tablespoon roughly chopped **fresh flat-leaf parsley**

1 tablespoon roughly chopped **fresh tarragon**

100g (3½oz) **mayonnaise**

1 tablespoon **small capers**

extra virgin olive oil

2 **endives** (optional)

8 **anchovy fillets** (optional)

salt and **freshly ground black pepper**

This recipe is from Jane's friend Sylvain – the founder chef of Root Camp UK, a hands-on cookery course for 14–21-year-olds. They taught this recipe to teenagers because it's a great way to develop knife skills. Chop chop.

Cook the peas in boiling water for a minute, or until tender. Scoop them out of the water and set to one side to cool. Add the carrots and potatoes to the same water, along with a teaspoon of salt, and cook for 15–25 minutes, or until the vegetables have started to soften.

Dice the carrots and potatoes into 1cm (½ inch) cubes. Transfer them to a large mixing bowl and add the red onion, peas, vinegar and herbs.

Add the mayonnaise, capers and a good drizzle of olive oil. Fold all the ingredients together gently, taking care not to break up the potato cubes. Season well with salt and pepper.

To serve, spoon the salad into the middle of a large dish and surround with endive leaves. If you're using anchovy fillets, place one on each leaf.

MARCELLA'S RICE SALAD

SERVES 2
PREP TIME: 10 MINS · COOK TIME: 30 MINS
WF · GF · DF · V · Ve

50g (1¾oz) **raisins**

125g (4½oz) **brown jasmine rice** or **wholegrain mixed rice blend**

50g (1¾oz) **dried figs**, chopped

50g (1¾oz) whole **blanched almonds**, toasted

2 tablespoons chopped **fresh coriander**

2 tablespoons chopped **fresh mint**

1 teaspoon **pomegranate molasses**

a pinch of **cayenne pepper**

2 tablespoons **olive oil**, to serve

a large pinch of **sumac**, to serve

seeds from ½ **pomegranate**, to serve

salt and **freshly ground black pepper**

John ate this in Ibiza and loved it.

Cover the raisins with hot water to plump them up.

Cook the rice in 250ml (9fl oz) of simmering water for about 30 minutes, or according to the instructions on the packet, until it's just going soft. Drain well and leave to cool.

Mix the rice in a large bowl with the rest of the ingredients including the drained raisins. Season well and serve with a drizzle of oil, a sprinkle of sumac and the pomegranate seeds.

> **\\\\ TIP ////**
> Other dried fruit such as apricots or dates could be used in this salad.

(STRICTLY) CAESAR SALAD

1 large or 2 small **Romaine lettuce**

2–3 tablespoons **Caesar dressing**
(see page 219)

a handful of **croutons** (see page 214)

2 tablespoons **Parmesan**, finely grated

1 tablespoon chopped **fresh chives**

This has become the favourite salad of Natasha and Eleanor (John's daughters), and is now a Saturday night special, eaten in front of Strictly. Serving the lettuce in wedges makes it more aesthetically pleasing and a crunchy delight.

Slice the lettuce into thick wedges and drizzle with the dressing. Sprinkle with the croutons, Parmesan and chives.

TIP
You can add grilled chicken, bacon, shrimps, shiitake mushrooms or a couple of poached eggs – whatever takes your fancy.

COBB

60g (2¼oz) **bacon lardons**
1 tablespoon **olive oil**
1 **cooked chicken breast**
2 **boiled eggs**
1 **avocado**
2 **plum tomatoes**
70g (2½oz) **blue cheese**
2 **apples**
½ **cos lettuce**

DRESSING:
1 tablespoon **red wine vinegar**
3 tablespoons **olive oil**
1 teaspoon **honey**
a dash of **Worcestershire sauce**
salt and **freshly ground black pepper**

The only rule with this salad is that all the components should be chopped to an equal size, so that it can be eaten with a spoon. Feel free to free-style by adding other ingredients (or swapping out anything you want to substitute).

Cook the lardons in a frying pan with the olive oil for a few minutes until lightly browned and crisp. Remove with a slotted spoon on to some kitchen paper.

Mix together all the ingredients for the dressing.

Dice all the salad ingredients into 1–2cm (½–¾ inch) cubes.

Toss the cos lettuce in a little of the dressing and arrange on a plate. Keeping the ingredients separate, pile them around the lettuce and drizzle with the remaining dressing.

\\\\ TIP ////
This salad can also be served with ranch dressing (see page 216).

3 WAYS WITH MOZZARELLA

PEACH & PROSCIUTTO

SERVES 2
PREP TIME: 5 MINS
COOK TIME: 5 MINS
WF · GF

2 **peaches**
125g (4½oz) **mozzarella**, sliced or ripped
70g (2½oz) **rocket**
2 slices of **prosciutto**, ripped

DRESSING:
1 tablespoon **fresh basil**, shredded
1 tablespoon **fresh mint**, chopped
2 teaspoons **balsamic vinegar**
2 tablespoons **olive oil**
salt and **freshly ground black pepper**

If summer were a salad, it would be this salad. Fresh, fun and fragrant. It doesn't hurt to add a crisp glass of white wine to the ingredients. (For literal recipe readers, we don't mean pouring wine on to the plate.)

Heat a griddle pan until hot. Cut the peaches in half and remove the stones. Place them flesh side down on the hot griddle and cook for 2 minutes until they have score marks. Turn over and repeat. Remove them from the griddle and set to one side. Mix together all the dressing ingredients. Slice the peaches into chunks and arrange on a serving plate with the mozzarella, rocket and prosciutto. Drizzle with the dressing.

FENNEL, TARRAGON & BOTTARGA

SERVES 2
PREP TIME: 10 MINS
WF · GF · V (with no bottarga)

2 **celery sticks**, thinly sliced
1 **fennel bulb**, trimmed and shaved
1 teaspoon **fennel seeds**, roughly ground
2 teaspoons **fresh tarragon**, chopped
2 teaspoons **salted capers**, rinsed and chopped
2 tablespoons **olive oil**
150g (5½oz) **mozzarella**
bottarga, grated (optional)
extra virgin olive oil
salt and **freshly ground black pepper**

In the eleventh century, a man called Simon Seth (Simon Seth, put your hands on your head) said bottarga was to be 'avoided totally'. We disagree. It's also nice on its own with just mozzarella.

Arrange the sliced and shaved vegetables on a serving plate. Whisk together the fennel seeds, tarragon, capers and oil. Season and drizzle the mixture over the fennel and celery. Arrange the mozzarella over the top and finish with a good grating of bottarga (if using) and a drizzle of extra virgin olive oil.

TOMATO & BASIL

SERVES 2
PREP TIME: 5 MINS
WF · GF · V

200g (7oz) good **tomatoes**, cored and thinly sliced
1 small **shallot**, finely diced
½ clove of **garlic**, crushed to a paste with salt
fresh basil leaves
3 tablespoons **olive oil**
1 tablespoon **red wine vinegar**
125g (4½oz) **mozzarella**
salt

This Italian gem is referred to either as the Caprese salad (it's from the island of Capri, where John once kissed Katie Ferryman on a school trip) or the Tricolour salad. It's thought by some that it was a patriotic invention made to represent the Italian flag. Either way, it will transport you to the Med for even less than Ryanair. And without the delays.

Mix the tomatoes, shallot, garlic paste, basil leaves, oil and vinegar together. Season with salt to taste. Place the mozzarella on top and mix through, or serve on the side. Eat immediately.

CHARGRILLED CHICKEN & CHORIZO CLUB CLASSIC

SERVES 2
PREP TIME: 10 MINS
WF · GF

100g (3½oz) **mixed salad leaves** (we use a combination of **spinach**, **cos lettuce** and **rocket**)

2–3 **chargrilled chicken thighs**

100g (3½oz) **frozen peas**, defrosted

100g (3½oz) **cooked quinoa**, cooled

50g (1¾oz) **chorizo**, sliced

1 **piquillo pepper**, cut into strips

1 tablespoon **aïoli** or **garlic mayo**

3 tablespoons **French vinaigrette** (see page 216)

This is one of our bestsellers. We also serve the club toppings on a rice box, which you can do at home easily with some brown rice and our Leon slaw (see page 194). Join the club. Tuck in.

Assemble this salad in layers – starting with the leaves, peas and quinoa and then topping with everything else.

\\\\ TIP ////
Chargrilled chicken thighs are available from many supermarket deli counters or you use the chicken breasts from very peri-peri chicken (see page 181) instead.

NATURALLY FAST

SNIP-IT SALAD

SERVES 2
PREP TIME: 20 MINS · COOK TIME: 10 MINS
WF · GF · V

3 **parsnips**, peeled and shaved

2 tablespoons **olive oil**

a pinch of **saffron**

1 **leek**, trimmed, cleaned and thinly sliced

1 **red apple**, cored and chopped

30g (1oz) **walnuts**, toasted and chopped

1 tablespoon **fresh chives**, chopped

50g (1¾oz) **watercress**

salt and **freshly ground black pepper**

DRESSING:

200g (7oz) **plain yoghurt**

1 tablespoon **walnut oil**

2 teaspoons **maple syrup**

a pinch of **ground cinnamon**

a pinch of **ground cumin**

2 tablespoons **lemon juice**

One to fill up on in the autumn months.

Shave the parsnips into long strips using a vegetable peeler, right down to the core. Heat the oil in a large pan with the saffron. Tip in the parsnip strips and stir-fry for a few minutes. Turn down the heat, cover and allow to cook for 5 minutes. Season and tip into a large bowl. Add the sliced leeks and stir to combine – the leeks do not need additional cooking. Leave to cool.

Add the rest of the ingredients, apart from the watercress, to the parsnips and leeks.

Whisk together the dressing ingredients and fold into the salad. Season well.

Arrange the watercress on a serving plate and top with the salad.

TIP

If you can't source walnut oil, you can substitute another nut oil.

KEEN-BEAN QUINOA

SERVES 2
PREP TIME: 10 MINS
WF · GF · DF · V · Ve

100g (3½oz) **cooked quinoa**, cooled
150g (5½oz) **cooked edamame beans**
250g (9oz) mix of **cooked peas,** sliced **raw sugar snaps,** sliced **broad beans** and sliced **French beans**
salt and **freshly ground black pepper**

DRESSING:
1 clove of **garlic**, crushed
1 tablespoon **white wine vinegar**
1 teaspoon **maple syrup**
3 tablespoons **olive oil**
2 tablespoons **mixed chopped fresh herbs: tarragon, chives, chervil** and **basil**

Fresh and fast.

Mix the quinoa in a large bowl with the beans and peas and season well.

Mix together the dressing ingredients and stir through the salad.

\\\ TIP ///
This salad could be made with other dressings, like the Leon tamari & sesame or the Middle Eastern dressing (see page 216).

WATERMELON & FETA

SERVES 2
PREP TIME: 10 MINS
WF · GF · V

400g (14oz) **watermelon**, cut into 3–4cm (1¼–1½ inch) chunks

2 tablespoons **marinated red onions** (see page 218)

60g (2¼oz) **feta**, crumbled

2 tablespoons **toasted pumpkin seeds**

10 **black olives**

2 tablespoons shredded **fresh mint**

50g (1¾oz) **rocket**

salt and **freshly ground black pepper**

extra virgin olive oil, to serve

A very grown-up fruit salad. Best eaten outside, in the sunshine, wearing a Hawaiian shirt, with pink wine. This one's for Glenn, the Leon Operations Director.

Arrange all the ingredients together on a serving plate. Season well and drizzle with olive oil.

TIP
To toast your own pumpkin seeds, dry-fry them until they start to pop.

FAGIOLI E TONNO

SERVES 2
PREP TIME: 10 MINS
WF · GF · DF

250g (9oz) **cannellini beans**, cooked and drained well

120g (4¼oz) **tinned tuna**, drained

1 **red onion**, chopped

2 cloves of **garlic**, crushed

1 tablespoon **red wine vinegar**

2 tablespoons **olive oil**

2 tablespoons roughly chopped **fresh flat-leaf parsley**, plus extra leaves to garnish

2 **celery sticks**, finely chopped

salt and **freshly ground black pepper**

That's a tuna and bean salad in Inglaterra-ish. Proper exotic, like. If you can use cooked dried beans the result will be better, but if you're in a hurry rinsed and drained tinned beans will make a good salad. Pole and line caught tinned tuna is the most ethical option. Save the dolphins.

Mix all the ingredients together and season well. Garnish with extra parsley.

\ \ \ \ TIP / / / ,

TO COOK DRIED CANNELLINI BEANS:

• Soak overnight in plenty of cold water.

• Drain well, then place in a pan and cover with fresh water. Add a few whole cloves of garlic, a sprig of fresh rosemary and a few cherry tomatoes.

• Bring to the boil, then simmer for about an hour or until just tender. Drain, season well and toss with olive oil.

CHICKEN & RICE NOODLE SALAD

SERVES 2
PREP TIME: 10 MINS · COOK TIME: 5 MINS
WF · GF · DF

50g (1¾oz) **rice noodles**

1 **chicken breast**, cooked and shredded

1 **carrot**, grated

6 **spring onions**, chopped

¼ of a **cucumber**, cut into batons

¼ of a **Chinese cabbage**, shredded

1 tablespoon chopped **fresh coriander, mint** and **basil**

1 tablespoon **black sesame seeds**

DRESSING:

1 **red chilli**, chopped

1 clove of **garlic**, crushed

2 tablespoons **lime juice**

2 tablespoons **fish sauce**

2 tablespoons **rapeseed oil**

1 tablespoon **palm sugar**

This tangy dressing is lick-the-bowl worthy. Taste the tang. This is for you, Lob.

Cook the rice noodles according to the instructions on the packet. Refresh with cold water and drain well. Roughly cut the noodles into 4–5cm (1½–2 inch) lengths. Place in a large bowl.

Add the rest of the ingredients to the noodles. Whisk together the dressing ingredients and add to the bowl. Toss together and adjust the seasoning to taste.

\\\\| TIP |///

Fried tofu could be added instead of or as well as the chicken. To make it totally veggie, use 1 tablespoon of tamarind paste instead of fish sauce.

TEMPEH & TOASTED TORTILLA

SERVES 2
PREP TIME: 15 MINS · COOK TIME: 10 MINS
DF · V · Ve

60g (2¼oz) **tempeh**, chopped

120g (4¼oz) **black beans**, drained

100g (3½oz) **cooked edamame beans**

1 **cooked cob of sweetcorn**, kernels removed

½ an **avocado**, chopped

½ an **orange** or **red pepper**, chopped

2 **corn tortillas**

salt and **freshly ground black pepper**

DRESSING:

3 tablespoons **olive oil**

1 tablespoon **lime juice**

1 **red chilli**, chopped

1 clove of **garlic**, crushed

2 tablespoons chopped **fresh coriander**

Tempeh, fermented soy, is a nutritious high-protein staple and it's easy on your digestion. It absorbs flavour really well and makes a welcome change from tofu. (No, sorry, no Tiny Tempeh jokes here. We are stronger than that.)

Heat the oven to 160°C/325°F/Gas Mark 3.

In a large bowl, mix together all the salad ingredients except the tortillas.

Cut the tortillas into thin strips. Toast in the oven for about 10 minutes until the strips are golden brown and crisp. Remove from the oven and set aside.

While the tortillas are toasting, mix together your dressing ingredients and toss with the salad. Season well and top with the crunchy tortilla strips.

⟍⟍\ TIP /⟋⟋

To cook the fresh corn, boil it for 10 minutes, then slice off the kernels. Alternatively, you can use tinned or frozen sweetcorn. You can also throw the tempeh in the oven with the tortillas if you'd rather it was warm.

CRAB WITH PINK GRAPEFRUIT

SERVES 2
PREP TIME: 15 MINS
DF

150g (5½oz) **white crabmeat**
1 tablespoon **olive oil**
1 tablespoon **lemon juice**
cayenne pepper, to season
1 **pink grapefruit**, segmented
1 **avocado**, chopped
50g (1¾oz) **watercress**
1 tablespoon chopped **fresh chives**
salt and **freshly ground black pepper**

Dressing:
2 tablespoons **mayonnaise**
4 **spring onions**, greens only, finely
chopped
1–2cm (½–¾ inch) piece of **ginger**,
peeled and finely grated
1 teaspoon **soy sauce**
1 teaspoon **rice vinegar**

John would like to dedicate this to Katie as an apology for losing his wedding ring in the sand castle at the Crab Shack in St Brelade's Bay, Jersey. And to the Pennys for helping to try to find it.

Season the crabmeat with the oil, lemon, salt and cayenne pepper.

Arrange the crab on a serving plate with the other salad ingredients.

For the dressing, blend the mayonnaise with the spring onions, ginger, soy and vinegar. Season well and serve on the side.

\\\\ TIP ////
Add some brown crabmeat to
the dressing if you like.

COURGETTI WITH TRAPANESE PESTO & HARD RICOTTA

SERVES 2
PREP TIME: 15 MINS · COOK TIME: 2 MINS
WF · GF · V

3 **courgettes**

1 tablespoon **olive oil**

salt and **freshly ground black pepper**

2 tablespoons grated **ricotta salata**, to serve

PESTO:

2 cloves of **garlic**, crushed

50g (1¾oz) **flaked almonds**, toasted

leaves from a small bunch of **fresh basil**

3 tablespoons **olive oil**

200g (7oz) **tomatoes**, skinned and chopped

2 tablespoons grated **pecorino**

salt and **freshly ground black pepper**

This is pasta on a health kick. The Sicilian pesto is silly good. If you can't get hold of a spiralizer, just use a vegetable peeler.

Using a spiralizer, make long strips – 'courgetti' – with the courgettes. Heat the oil in a large frying pan and toss the courgette strips in it for a minute. Season well and transfer to a large bowl.

In a pestle and mortar or a food processor, make a paste with the garlic, almonds, basil and olive oil. Add the chopped tomatoes and crush them a little to combine with the paste. Stir in the pecorino and season.

Toss the courgette strips with the pesto and top with the grated ricotta salata.

TIP
Feta can be used instead of the ricotta salata.

BROWN SHRIMP & PINK PEPPERCORN

SERVES 2
PREP TIME: 15 MINS (plus salting) • **COOK TIME: 5 MINS**
WF · GF · DF

¼ of a **cucumber**, thinly sliced

2 **leeks**, sliced across

100g (3½oz) **brown shrimps**

finely grated **nutmeg**

a pinch of **cayenne pepper**

1 **hard-boiled egg**

2 **radishes**, finely chopped

1 tablespoon chopped **fresh dill**

2 teaspoons **pink peppercorns**

½ clove of **garlic**, crushed

2 tablespoons **olive oil**

1 tablespoon **lemon juice**

salt

Both of us love this salad – variants of it are staples in our houses. Jane loves using it as part of an antipasti spread. John last made it in a small galley on a boat in Cowes – he had to add some crayfish as the shops were shut, which worked OK.

Sprinkle the cucumber slices with a little salt, mix around, and leave in a colander for 15 minutes.

Steam the leeks for 5 minutes until they're just cooked. Season and leave to cool. Arrange the salted cucumber on a plate. Top with the leeks and shrimps. Season with lots of grated nutmeg, cayenne and salt. Grate the egg over the top and sprinkle with the radishes and dill.

In a pestle and mortar, crush the peppercorns with the garlic. Add the olive oil and lemon juice, mix well and pour over the salad.

\\\ TIP ///

Pink peppercorns aren't really peppercorns (liars). They're a dried berry with a delicately peppery taste. Use black peppercorns if you can't find them. Salting cucumber brings out lots of the liquid – stopping soggy, watery hell.

HISPI, PROSCIUTTO & PARMESAN

SERVES 2
PREP TIME: 10 MINS
WF · GF

¼ **Hispi cabbage**, shredded

1 **fennel bulb**, shaved

4 thin slices of **prosciutto**, roughly shaved

30g **Parmesan**, shaved, plus extra to serve

2 tablespoons good **balsamic vinegar**

2 tablespoons **olive oil**

salt and **freshly ground black pepper**

A naturally fast salad in its element. A simple assembly job.

Toss everything together in a large bowl and season well.

TIP
For crisp wafer-thin fennel, shave on a mandolin and leave in iced water until needed.

GREEN, EGGS & HAM

SERVES 2
PREP TIME: 15 MINS • COOK TIME: 5 MINS
WF • GF • DF

200g (7oz) **celeriac**, cut into thin
    matchsticks

1 **apple**, chopped

2 tablespoons **mustard mayonnaise**
    (see page 218)

1 tablespoon chopped **fresh tarragon,
    chives** and **parsley**

1 tablespoon chopped **capers**

1 tablespoon chopped **gherkins**

1 clove of **garlic**, crushed

1 **shallot**, finely chopped

about 120g (4¼oz) good-quality **ham
    hock**, roughly shredded

2 **boiled eggs**, quartered

50g (1¾oz) **lamb's lettuce** or **purslane**

salt and **freshly ground black pepper**

You can use red apples too. It just sounds so much better this way.

Mix all the ingredients except for the ham, eggs and leaves in a large bowl and season well.

Arrange, stylishly, on a serving plate with the ham hock, boiled eggs and lamb's lettuce.

＼＼＼ TIP ／／／
You can use some nice ham if you
prefer it to ham hock.

MIDDLE EASTERN SPICED QUINOA

SERVES 2

PREP TIME: 10 MINS

WF · GF · DF · V · Ve

200g (7oz) **cooked quinoa**, cooled

1 **carrot**, grated

1 **avocado**, diced

100g (3½oz) **cooked edamame beans**

2 tablespoons **pistachios**, chopped

6 **dried apricots**, chopped

salt and **freshly ground black pepper**

DRESSING:

3 tablespoons **olive oil**

1 tablespoon **pomegranate molasses**

1 tablespoon **lemon juice**

a pinch of **sumac**

1 tablespoon chopped **fresh dill** and **mint**

A rich, simple salad. Make double the amount and take it into the office to be the envy of your desk cluster.

Mix the salad ingredients together in a bowl.

Whisk together the dressing and toss it with the salad. Season well.

\\\\ TIP ////

TO COOK QUINOA WELL:

- Always rinse in lots of cold water and drain well.
- Leave to dry for about 10 minutes. Toast quinoa first in a little oil over a medium heat before adding the liquid.
- Add 1.5 parts liquid to 1 part quinoa. Chicken or veg stock can be used.
- Cook for 15 minutes and leave for 10 before fluffing up.

FRIED HALLOUMI & AVOCADO

SERVES 2
PREP TIME: 15 MINS · COOK TIME: 5 MINS
WF · GF · V (only **GF** if no pitta)

100g (3½oz) **halloumi**

1 tablespoon **olive oil**

150g (5½oz) **tomatoes**

1 **avocado**

2 **Little Gem lettuces**

2 tablespoons **hummus**

salt and **freshly ground black pepper**

2 **pitta breads**, to serve (optional)

DRESSING:

2 tablespoons **almonds**, toasted
   and chopped

1 **piquillo pepper**, finely chopped

1 tablespoon **balsamic vinegar**

3 tablespoons **olive oil**

1 tablespoon chopped **fresh chives**

1 teaspoon **maple syrup**

Fried cheese doesn't really need an introduction. You know you'll like it. Serve as a salad or stuff in a pitta bread.

Slice the halloumi into pieces about 1cm (½ inch) thick. Dry well with kitchen paper. Heat the oil in a non-stick pan and fry the halloumi slices for 2 minutes on each side until golden brown. Remove from the pan and drain on kitchen paper.

Slice the tomatoes and avocado. Cut the Little Gem into 6 wedges and griddle them until charred. Whisk together all the dressing ingredients and season well.

Arrange all the vegetables on a plate, and season well. Dollop the hummus around, and top with the halloumi pieces. Drizzle the dressing over the salad and serve with pittas, if liked.

\\\\ TIP ////

Spanish piquillo peppers are a great storecupboard ingredient and can be used chopped in salads or puréed and stirred into dressings.

CARRY AWAY MACKEREL

SERVES 2
PREP TIME: 15 MINS · COOK TIME: 2 MINS
WF · GF

¼ of a **Hispi cabbage**, shredded

½ large **beetroot**, grated

2 tablespoons marinated **red onions** (see page 218)

1 tablespoon **caraway seeds**

2 tablespoons **sauerkraut**

a 2cm (¾ inch) square piece of **fresh horseradish**, finely grated

1 tablespoon **soured cream** (or **crème fraîche**)

150g (5½oz) good **smoked mackerel**, flaked

1 tablespoon chopped **fresh chives**

salt and **freshly ground black pepper**

Carry this salad to the garden, and eat it on a blanket. Careful not to spill any, though, or you may have some pungent picnics in the future.

Mix the cabbage, beetroot and marinated red onions together in a large bowl.

Heat a small pan and toast the caraway seeds until fragrant. Tip into a pestle and mortar and grind roughly. Add to the salad bowl.

Add the rest of the ingredients, season well and fold together.

\ \ \ \ **TIP** / / / /
Creamed horseradish can be used instead of fresh. Just add to taste.

ACQUA E SALE

SERVES 2
PREP TIME: 15 MINS
DF · V · Ve

200g (9oz) **cherry tomatoes**, halved

1 clove of **garlic**, crushed

2 tablespoons **marinated red onions** (see page 218)

½ **cucumber**, peeled, deseeded, cut into 4 lengthways, then into 1cm (½ inch) pieces

1 tablespoon chopped **fresh flat-leaf parsley**

a good pinch of **dried oregano**

a very good slug of **extra virgin olive oil**

150g **stale sourdough** or **ciabatta**, ripped into small pieces

salt and **freshly ground black pepper**

Originating from Puglia, this is twist on a panzanella, which is traditionally made to use up leftovers. 'Water and salt', and a few other things too.

Mix the tomatoes with the garlic, red onions, cucumber, parsley and oregano. Season well and coat with olive oil.

Sprinkle the bread pieces with 50ml (2fl oz) of water and fold into the vegetables. Drizzle with more oil and season again.

\\\\ TIP ////

This goes really well with buffalo mozzarella or burrata.

PASTRAMI SALADWICH

SERVES 2
PREP TIME: 15 MINS · COOK TIME: 2 MINS
WF · GF · DF

¼ of a **Savoy cabbage**, shredded

150g (5½oz) **celeriac**, grated

1 large **carrot**, grated

100g (3½oz) **pastrami**, cut into thin strips

4 **spring onions**, chopped

1 tablespoon chopped **fresh chives**

DRESSING:

2 tablespoons **olive oil**

2 tablespoons **black mustard seeds**

2 teaspoons **English mustard**

1 clove of **garlic**, crushed

1 tablespoon **cider vinegar**

salt and **freshly ground black pepper**

A deconstructed, jazzed-up sandwich.

Place all the salad ingredients in a large bowl and mix well.

Heat the oil in a small frying pan. Add the mustard seeds, and when they start to pop, remove the pan from the heat and add the rest of the dressing ingredients. Whisk to combine. Season well and toss the dressing with the salad.

> ＼＼＼ **TIP** ／／／
> Use your leftover cabbage and celeriac to make a slaw with the mustard dressing. You can use salt beef or bresaola if you can't find pastrami.

SQUID ORZO SALAD

SERVES 2
PREP TIME: 10 MINS · COOK TIME: 12 MINS
DF

100g (3½oz) **orzo pasta**

1½ tablespoons of **olive oil**

200g (7oz) cleaned **squid**, tubes opened flat

chilli parsley garlic dressing (see page 218)

50g (1¾oz) **rocket**

salt and **freshly ground black pepper**

See this seafood on your plate in a flash. This salad will bring you good luck. Orzo they say.

Cook the pasta as per the instructions on the packet. Drain well and drizzle with a tablespoon of olive oil.

Heat a griddle pan until very hot. Toss the squid in the remaining oil and season well. Grill on the pan for a couple of minutes on each side, depending on the size of the squid. Cook the tentacles for a little longer, about 2 minutes. Remove and leave to cool. Cut the squid into slices.

Whisk together the dressing ingredients and toss the pasta with the dressing, squid and rocket. Season well.

\\\\ TIP ////

You can buy packs of frozen cleaned squid. If you can't get your hands on orzo, any other small pasta will do, and Israeli couscous would also work.

CAUCHOISE

SERVES 2

PREP TIME: 10 MINS · COOK TIME: 20 MINS

WF · GF

200g (7oz) **new potatoes**

3 **celery sticks**, sliced

1 tablespoon chopped **fresh tarragon**, **chervil** and **chives**

2 tablespoons **crème fraîche**

4 **spring onions**, chopped

50g (1¾oz) **watercress**

50g (1¾oz) **ham**, cut into thin strips

DRESSING:

1 teaspoon **Dijon mustard**

1 tablespoon **cider vinegar**

1 clove of **garlic**, crushed

3 tablespoons **rapeseed oil**

salt and **freshly ground black pepper**

This is a traditional salad from Pays de Caux in Normandy. It's big, satisfying and really fun to say.

Cook the potatoes in boiling water until they're just tender. While they're cooking, whisk together the dressing ingredients and season well.

Drain the potatoes thoroughly and toss, while still hot, in the salad dressing. Leave to cool. When cool enough to handle, cut the potatoes into chunks or slices and leave them in the dressing.

Fold the potato mixture with the celery, herbs, crème fraîche and spring onions. Serve on a bed of watercress, topped with the ham strips.

BELGIAN STEAK

SERVES 2
PREP TIME: 15 MINS · COOK TIME: 8 MINS
WF · GF · DF

1 **chicory head**, finely sliced

¼ of a **radicchio head**, finely sliced

1 **leek**, finely sliced

200–250g (7–9oz) **sirloin steak** (or another cut)

1 tablespoon **olive oil**

100g (3½oz) **chestnut mushrooms**, sliced

salt and **freshly ground black pepper**

DRESSING:

2 tablespoons **mustard mayonnaise** (see page 218)

1 tablespoon chopped **chives**

Steak-frites is said to be Belgium's national dish. This recipe doesn't have any chips, but we won't stop you serving them on the side.

Mix together the chicory, radicchio and leek in a large bowl.

Heat a griddle pan until it's very hot. Brush the steak with a little olive oil, and season well. Cook for a couple of minutes on each side and remove to a plate to rest, uncovered.

Add the mushrooms to the same pan, brown them for a few minutes, then set to one side.

Dress the chicory mix with the mustard mayonnaise, then add the chives and season. Toss through the cooled mushrooms. Slice the steak and pop on top of the dressed salad.

\\\ **TIP** ///
Use leftover roast beef in this salad if you have any.

PINK QUINOA

SERVES 1

PREP TIME: 10 MINS

WF · GF · DF · V · Ve (not DF or Ve if topped with halloumi crumbs)

200g (9oz) **cooked quinoa**, cooled

100g (3½oz) **cooked beetroot**

2 teaspoons **pomegranate molasses**

juice of ½ an **orange**

1 tablespoon **olive oil**

½ a clove of **garlic**, crushed

¼ **pomegranate**, seeds only

3 **radishes**, sliced

½ **red onion**, chopped

a pinch of **sumac**

salt and **freshly ground black pepper**

TO SERVE:

roasted halloumi crumbs (optional, see page 215)

Don't worry, pink quinoa is not a new type of quinoa you haven't heard of before. It's pink because of the beetroot. It's still trusty ol' quinoa.

Place the quinoa in a bowl.

Make the beetroot dressing by blitzing the next 5 ingredients together using a stick blender, and season well.

Fold the dressing through the quinoa and add the rest of the ingredients.

\\\\ TIP ////

Beetroot can be cooked quickly by peeling, grating and cooking in a little oil for 10 minutes. It's not the beetroot of all evil.

VEGETABLE FREEKEH WITH DATE YOGHURT

SERVES 1

PREP TIME: 15 MINS · COOK TIME: 40 MINS

V

2 **parsnips**

2 **carrots**

2 tablespoons **olive oil**

100g (3½oz) **freekeh** (or **smoked freekeh**)

salt and **freshly ground black pepper**

DRESSING:

grated zest and juice of ½ an **orange**

½ a clove of **garlic**, crushed

2 tablespoons **plain yoghurt**

a pinch of **ground cumin** and **cardamom**

4 **dates**, pitted and finely chopped

1 **red chilli**, finely chopped

1 teaspoon **honey**

1 teaspoon chopped **fresh mint**

TO SERVE:

a bunch of **watercress**

pomegranate seeds

chopped **fresh mint**

za'atar

If you're making it the night before, leave the watercress and garnish separate until you're just about to tuck in.

Heat the oven to 190°C/375°F/Gas Mark 5.

Peel the parsnips and carrots and cut into quarters lengthways. Toss in 1 tablespoon of olive oil. Season well and roast on a baking tray for about 40 minutes until tender.

Meanwhile, wash and cook the freekeh as per instructions on the packet. Drain well and toss in the remaining tablespoon of olive oil. Season while still warm.

To make the dressing, place all the ingredients in a bowl and whisk to combine, seasoning with salt and pepper.

To assemble the salad, gently fold the roasted veg with the freekeh and watercress. Arrange on a serving plate. Drizzle with the yoghurt dressing and sprinkle with pomegranate seeds, chopped mint and za'atar.

\\\\ TIP ////

For a change, blanch the vegetable wedges in boiling water for a few minutes. Drain and toss in olive oil. Grill on a hot griddle until lightly browned and add to the salad. Other vegetables could be used instead, such as squash, pumpkin and celeriac.

CURED MACKEREL

150g (5½oz) **mackerel fillets**, pin-boned
1 teaspoon **salt**
50ml (2fl oz) **water**
50ml (2fl oz) **white wine vinegar**
25g (1oz) **brown sugar**
50g (1¾oz) **cooked peas**
10 small **gherkins**, sliced
1 **shallot**, chopped
1 tablespoon **olive oil**
1 tablespoon chopped **fresh dill**
150g **Israeli couscous**, cooked
a handful of **lamb's lettuce**
salt and **freshly ground black pepper**
extra virgin olive oil

The mackerel is cured. Rejoice.

· ·

Dry the mackerel well with kitchen paper and sprinkle with the salt. Leave for about 20 minutes. Wipe any excess salt from the fillets and dry them again. Put them into a bowl. Heat up the measured water and vinegar with the sugar until the sugar has dissolved and the liquid is hot. Pour it over the fish and leave to 'cook'.

Remove the fish from the liquid after a few minutes, when it has just cooked (this will depend on the thickness of the fillets) and dry well on kitchen paper. Slice into pieces on the diagonal.

Mix the peas, gherkins, shallot, oil and dill together and season well. Fold in the mackerel. On a plate, arrange the couscous and the lamb's lettuce. Top with the mackerel and peas and drizzle with extra virgin oil.

TIP
Fried or smoked mackerel can be used in this salad for speed. Other cooked oily fish can be used too.

HOT-SMOKED SALMON

1 small **raw beetroot**, peeled and coarsely grated

2 tablespoons **olive oil**

½ a clove of **garlic**, crushed

1 teaspoon **caraway seeds**

finely grated zest and juice of ½ an **orange**

1 teaspoon **balsamic vinegar**

2cm (¾ inch) piece of **cucumber**

4 **radishes**

200g **freekeh**, cooked

100g **hot-smoked salmon**, in one piece

a handful **watercress**

1 tablespoon roughly chopped **fresh dill**

salt and **freshly ground black pepper**

DRESSING:

1 tablespoon **crème fraîche**

1 teaspoon **lemon juice**

2 teaspoons grated **horseradish** (or **hot horseradish cream**)

TIP

Cold-smoked salmon or any other smoked fish, like eel, for those of you who are more adventurous, can be used instead of hot-smoked salmon.

This salad makes you want to live for a long time. It will probably help you do so.

Place the grated beetroot in a bowl. Make an orange dressing by heating half the oil in a small pan, then adding the garlic and caraway seeds. Before the garlic colours, tip in the orange zest and juice and cook for 5 minutes, or until the orange has reduced to a syrupy consistency. Mix in the balsamic vinegar and the remaining olive oil. Dress the beetroot with the orange dressing, season well and mix thoroughly.

Mix the horseradish dressing ingredients together in a bowl, whisking well to combine. Add a little water to bring it to the consistency of double cream. Set to one side to let the flavours develop.

Prepare the cucumber and radishes by slicing thinly into rounds, then cutting across the rounds into thin matchsticks.

Gently pull the salmon into large chunks and place on top of the dressed beetroot and freekeh. Drizzle with the horseradish dressing and sprinkle the cucumber, radishes and watercress. Top with dill.

GIANT COUSCOUS

SERVES 1
PREP TIME: 15 MINS · COOK TIME: 10 MINS
DF · V · Ve

150g (5½oz) **cooked giant couscous**, cooled

1 **courgette**

¼ of an **aubergine**

1 tablespoon **olive oil**

6 **cherry tomatoes**, quartered

1 **piquillo pepper**, cut into strips

basil dressing (see page 216)

salt and **freshly ground black pepper**

This ginormous salad will keep you full without making you feel stodgy. Making it simple to dine-at-desk.

Place the couscous in a large bowl. Cut the courgette and aubergine into either chunks or strips. The chunks can be fried in the olive oil until tender; the strips can be grilled on a griddle pan.

Toss the cooked veg with the couscous along with the tomatoes and pepper strips.

Fold the basil dressing into the salad and season well.

\\\\ TIP ////

Don't be afraid to poke your veg. You can press them to feel whether they are cooked or not when they're on the griddle pan.

Pine nuts, semi-dried tomatoes and shaved fennel could also be added to the couscous.

SPICED TEMPEH & KALE

SERVES 1
PREP TIME: 15 MINS · COOK TIME: 15 MINS
DF · V · Ve

100g (3½oz) **kale**, stems removed

2 teaspoons **sesame oil**

50g (1¾oz) **cooked tempeh**

1 tablespoon **rapeseed oil**

1 teaspoon **chilli sauce**

2 teaspoons **soy sauce**

a pinch of **cayenne pepper**

1 **carrot**, grated

50g (1¾oz) **cooked sweetcorn kernels**

2 tablespoons **roasted chickpeas**
   (see page 215)

1 tablespoon **toasted sesame seeds**

salt and **freshly ground black pepper**

DRESSING:

½ a clove of **garlic**, crushed

1 tablespoon **rice vinegar**

1 tablespoon **sesame oil**

1 tablespoon **rapeseed oil**

1 teaspoon finely grated **ginger**

TO SERVE:

1 tablespoon chopped **fresh coriander**

Crisp up the chickpeas in the oven at the same time as you are cooking the kale. They both make great 'bar snacks' on their own too.

Heat the oven to 150°C/300°F/Gas Mark 2.

Toss the kale in the sesame oil, season and spread out over a baking tray. Cook for about 10–15 minutes in the oven until crisp and slightly browned around the edges.

Finely slice the tempeh. Heat the rapeseed oil in a small frying pan. When hot, add the tempeh and stir-fry for 1 minute. Quickly add the chilli sauce, soy sauce and cayenne pepper. Toss until coated, then remove from the heat.

In a large bowl, mix the kale, carrot, sweetcorn, chickpeas and sesame seeds. Whisk together the dressing ingredients and mix with the salad. Season well. Top with the tempeh pieces and chopped coriander.

\\\ TIP ///

If you've bought raw tempeh, cook it for 20 minutes before using. Extra spices like cumin and coriander can be added to the tempeh to flavour it.

3 WAYS WITH CAULIFLOWER

SAFFRON-ROASTED

SERVES 1
PREP TIME: 15 MINS
COOK TIME: 20 MINS
WF · GF · DF · V · Ve

¼ of a **cauliflower**
½ a **romanesco**
1 tablespoon **olive oil**
1 tablespoon **sultanas**
50g (1¾oz) **kale**, cooked and chopped
1 **shallot**, chopped
1 tablespoon chopped **fresh flat-leaf parsley**
1 tablespoon **pine nuts**, toasted
salt and **freshly ground black pepper**

SAFFRON VINAIGRETTE:
a pinch of **saffron**, soaked in 1 tablespoon boiling water
1 tablespoon **sherry vinegar**
2 tablespoons **olive oil**
½ a clove of **garlic**, crushed
1 teaspoon **maple syrup**

We think you will love this. If you are feeling fancy and flush, buy Iranian saffron.

Heat the oven to 170°C/325°F/Gas Mark 3. Break the cauliflower and romanesco into florets. Toss in the olive oil, season well and bake in the oven for about 15–20 minutes, or until just starting to colour. Cover the sultanas with hot water. While the veg are cooking, make your saffron vinaigrette by whisking together the ingredients and seasoning with salt and pepper. Pour the dressing into a bowl. When the cauliflower and romanesco are cooked, tip them into the dressing while they're still hot. Stir well and leave to cool. Add the rest of the ingredients to the salad, including the drained sultanas.

BACON & WALNUT DRESSING

SERVES 1
PREP TIME: 15 MINS
COOK TIME: 20 MINS
WF · GF · DF

½ a **cauliflower**, broken into florets and roasted as in the previous recipe
1 **leek**, sliced and cooked
1 **celery stick**, sliced
50g (1¾oz) **cooked bacon lardons**
1 tablespoon chopped **fresh chives**
a handful of **baby spinach leaves**
2 tablespoons **walnut dressing** (see page 219)

You can make this veggie by leaving out the bacon.

Toss all the ingredients, apart from the spinach, with the dressing. Serve on the spinach leaves and sprinkle with chives.

\\\\ **TIP** ////
Roasting cauliflower is a revelation and a great way to intensify the flavour. When it comes out of the oven, try tossing it with a little grated cheese and leave to cool.

CAULI-COUS

SERVES 1
PREP TIME: 15 MINS
COOK TIME: 5 MINS
WF · GF · V

½ a **cauliflower**
1 tablespoon **olive oil**
2 tablespoons **marinated red onions** (see page 218)
5 **sunblush tomatoes**, chopped
¼ of a **cucumber**, chopped
10 **fresh basil leaves**, shredded
1 tablespoon **pine nuts**, toasted
1 tablespoon **feta**, crumbled
salt and **freshly ground black pepper**

A great way of eating gluten free.

Break the cauliflower into florets and blitz in a food processor until they resemble couscous. This can also be done by finely chopping. Heat the oil in a large shallow pan and cook the cauliflower for a few minutes, stirring constantly and seasoning well. Tip out into a bowl and add the rest of the ingredients.

BLACK RICED PEAS

SERVES 1
PREP TIME: 10 MINS · COOK TIME: 5 MINS
WF · GF · DF · V

150g (5½oz) **cooked black rice**

100g (3½oz) **cooked peas**

1 bunch of **spring onions**, chopped

1 **red chilli**, finely chopped

1 or 2 **boiled eggs**, depending on how hungry you are

1 tablespoon chopped **fresh coriander**

a handful of **pea shoots** (optional)

CURRY VINAIGRETTE:

1 teaspoon **curry powder**

1 tablespoon **rice vinegar**

2 tablespoons **rapeseed oil**

1 teaspoon finely grated **ginger**

salt and **freshly ground black pepper**

When testing recipes, Jane got so distracted eating this salad that she completely forgot to write down how to make it. Luckily she made and ate it a few more times, so it's here now.

Mix the rice in a large bowl with the peas, spring onions and chilli.

Whisk together the vinaigrette ingredients and season with salt and pepper.

Toss the dressing with the rice and top with the halved boiled eggs, coriander and pea shoots if using.

\\\ TIP ///

Cooked flaked smoked haddock would make a great addition.

KAREN'S SQUASH SALAD

SERVES 1
PREP TIME: 15 MINS · COOK TIME: 30 MINS
WF · GF · DF · V · Ve

200g (9oz) **squash**, cut into 2–3cm
  (¾–1¼ inch) chunks
1 tablespoon **olive oil**
1 teaspoon **garam masala**
1 **shallot**, finely chopped
50g (1¾oz) **piquillo peppers**, roughly
  chopped
2 tablespoons **cooked lentils**
2 tablespoons **chickpeas**, cooked or
  roasted (see page 215)
50g (1¾oz) **cooked peas** and **cooked
  broad beans**
1 tablespoon chopped **fresh mint** and
  chopped **fresh flat-leaf parsley**
2 tablespoons **sunflower seeds**, toasted
salt and **freshly ground black pepper**

DRESSING:
1 clove of **garlic**, crushed
2 tablespoons **olive oil**
1 tablespoon **cider vinegar**
½–1 **red chilli**, chopped
1 tablespoon **almonds**, chopped
2 **sun-dried tomatoes**, chopped
4 **olives**, chopped

Karen made this salad for a family lunch and Rachael, who works in our marketing team, loved it so much that it's made its way into this book. It rocks, and Karen rocks.

Heat the oven to 170°C/325°F/Gas Mark 3.

Toss the squash with the olive oil and garam masala. Season with salt and pepper, and roast in the oven for about 30 minutes, or until tender. Leave to cool, then mix in a large bowl with the next 5 ingredients.

Mix together the dressing ingredients, season and toss with the squash mix.

Just before serving, add the herbs and sunflower seeds.

\\\ TIP ///

The salad keeps well in the fridge for a couple of days, but try not to add the fresh herbs until just before serving. Lovely with lamb or just by itself, with salad leaves.

MALAYSIAN SALAD WITH IKAN BILIS

SERVES 1
PREP TIME: 15 MINS
DF

1 tablespoon **desiccated coconut**, toasted

2 teaspoons **dried prawns**, soaked in hot water

¼ of a **cucumber**, peeled, deseeded and cut into strips

50g (1¾oz) **beansprouts**

2 **spring onions**, chopped

100g **mixed veg (mangetout, sugar snaps, French** or **runner beans)**, all cut into strips

5 **fresh mint leaves**, shredded

1 **red chilli**, chopped

juice of ½ a **lime**

1 teaspoon *kecap manis*

½ teaspoon **palm sugar**

1 teaspoon **sesame oil**

salt and **freshly ground black pepper**

TO SERVE:
fresh chives
25g *ikan bilis* (see page 214)

Ikan bilis are salt-cured anchovies, and this salad is a cure for a dreary day. It's got a real depth of flavour, and the raw mixed veg give it a satisfying crunch.

Grind the toasted coconut in a pestle and mortar with the dried prawns.

In a bowl, mix all the prepared veg with the mint and chilli. Mix together the remaining ingredients and toss with the salad. Fold through the coconut prawn paste and season well.

Add the chives and *ikan bilis* and serve.

\\\\ TIP ////

Cooked prawns or other seafood could be added to this salad. Toasted coconut and the *kecap manis* dressing go surprisingly well with sliced tomatoes too.

KALE & PEANUT

More than the sum of its parts. Go on, all the kale kids are doing it.

100g (3½oz) **kale**

50g (1¾oz) **spring greens**

1 tablespoon chopped **fresh coriander**

a pinch of chopped **fresh mint**

3 tablespoons **Leon tamari & sesame dressing** (see page 216, make sure tamari is gluten free if you want a gluten-free salad)

1 tablespoon roasted **peanuts**, roughly chopped

Finely shred the kale and spring greens and mix with the herbs. Mix in the dressing and sprinkle with peanuts to serve.

KALE CAESAR

SERVES 1
PREP TIME: 10 MINS
WF · GF

100g (3½oz) **kale**, de-stemmed

50g (1¾oz) **spring greens**, de-stemmed

3 tablespoons **Leon honey & mustard dressing** (see page 218)

100g (3½oz) **cooked chicken**, shredded

4 **salted anchovies**, chopped

1 tablespoon finely grated **Parmesan**

1 tablespoon chopped **fresh chives**

Although this does not use a traditional Caesar dressing (see page 219), the anchovies and Parmesan make it highly reminiscent of one. People really do hail the kale at Leon.

Shred the kale and spring greens thinly. Toss with the dressing and top with the other ingredients to serve.

POLISH HERRING & POTATO SALAD

SERVES 1

PREP TIME: 15 MINS

WF · GF

100g (3½oz) **rollmops**, drained well
and sliced

100g (3½oz) **beetroot**, cooked and diced

100g (3½oz) **potatoes**, cooked and diced

½ an **apple**, diced

½ a **red onion**, sliced

1 teaspoon **hot horseradish cream**

1 tablespoon **soured cream**

1 tablespoon chopped **fresh dill**
and **chives**

red chicory leaves

salt and **freshly ground black pepper**

Rollmops are a lot nicer than they sound. Trust us.

Put the first 5 ingredients into a bowl and fold them together. Mix the horseradish cream with the soured cream and half the herbs. Season well.

Fold the cream into the salad. Arrange on the chicory leaves and sprinkle with the rest of the herbs.

TIP

You can serve this with grated hard-boiled eggs and sweet dill pickles. Or sprinkle fresh horseradish on top.

TOMATO, FETA & LENTIL

SERVES 1

PREP TIME: 10 MINS

WF · GF · V

100g (3½oz) **cooked lentils**

¼ **cucumber**, diced

1 tablespoon roughly chopped **fresh dill**

2 tablespoons **French vinaigrette** (see page 216)

3 **semi-dried tomatoes**, sliced

30g (1oz) **baby plum tomatoes**, halved

30g (1oz) **feta**, crumbled

a handful of **rocket**

1 tablespoon **Leon toasted seeds** (see page 215)

salt and **freshly ground black pepper**

We think this is an ideal midsummer salad. Lentils are fantastic for fuelling up long days, and even longer nights.

Mix the lentils with the cucumber and dill in a bowl. Season and dress with the vinaigrette.

Top with the other ingredients.

\\\\ VARIATIONS ////

RUBY MACKEREL:

WF · GF · DF

· Leave out the tomatoes and feta. Add 100g (3½oz) of flaked smoked mackerel and a tablespoon of pomegranate seeds and blueberries.

HAM HOCK & LENTIL:

WF · GF · DF

· Leave out the tomatoes and feta and replace with 100g (3½oz) of shredded ham hock. Serve with Leon honey & mustard dressing.

SUPERCLEAN CHICKEN & QUINOA

SERVES 1
PREP TIME: 15 MINS
WF · GF · DF

150g (5½oz) **cooked quinoa**

100g (3½oz) **cooked chicken breast**, chopped

4 **sun-dried tomatoes**, finely chopped

50g (1¾oz) **garden peas**, cooked

a 2–3cm (¾–1¼ inch) piece of **cucumber**, deseeded and chopped

1 tablespoon chopped **fresh mint** and **parsley**

2 tablespoons **olive oil**

1 tablespoon **lemon juice**

¼ of a **pomegranate**, seeds only

salt and **freshly ground black pepper**

a wedge of **lemon**, to serve

2015 at Leon was all about getting Lean and Clean. Not starving yourself, but giving your body the fuel it needs. Lean back, and enjoy.

In a large bowl, gently mix all the ingredients together except the pomegranate and lemon, which are used to top the salad after seasoning.

\ \ \ \ TIP / / / /

Leave out the chicken to make this a vegan salad. To up the good fats, you can add avocado.

CHICKEN WITH SWEETCORN DRESSING

SERVES 1
PREP TIME: 15 MINS
WF · GF · DF

100g (3½oz) **cooked chicken breast**, cut
   into strips

½ an **avocado**, sliced

6 **cherry tomatoes**, halved

4 **spring onions**, chopped

½ a **Little Gem lettuce**

50g (1¾oz) **black beans**, drained

DRESSING:

1 **cob of sweetcorn**, kernels removed and
   roughly chopped

½ a clove of **garlic**, crushed

1 **red chilli**, chopped

1 **shallot**, chopped

1 **piquillo pepper**, chopped

juice of ½ a **lime**

2 tablespoons **olive oil**

1 tablespoon chopped **fresh coriander**

salt and **freshly ground black pepper**

Beats chicken and sweetcorn sandwich filler, hands down. But you already knew that.

Arrange all the salad ingredients on a plate or in a jar if you're a hipster.

Mix together the dressing ingredients and season well. Drizzle over the salad.

TONNATO CHICKEN & ARTICHOKE

SERVES 1
PREP TIME: 15 MINS
WF · GF · DF

150g (5½oz) **cooked chicken**, thinly sliced

100g (3½oz) **cooked French beans**, trimmed

2 cooked **artichoke hearts**, sliced

¼ of a **cos lettuce**, shredded

DRESSING:
1 **anchovy fillet**
5 **capers**
leaves from a sprig of **fresh basil**
½ a clove of **garlic**, crushed
2 tablespoons **mayonnaise**
1 tablespoon **oil from tuna/anchovy**
1 tablespoon **tinned tuna**
salt and **freshly ground black pepper**

TO SERVE:
fresh basil leaves
anchovies
capers

Imagine you are driving through Italy, and you stop off at a small family restaurant for lunch. If you want to.

Arrange the chicken, beans, artichokes and cos lettuce on a plate, making sure that there are chicken slices visible.

In a pestle and mortar, crush the anchovy, capers, basil and garlic together to make a paste. A little salt will help to break the basil down.

Mix the paste with the mayonnaise and the oil. Stir in the tinned tuna. The mixture should have the consistency of double cream. If it is too thick, let it down with a little water, then season.

Drizzle the tonnato sauce over the salad and sprinkle with the extra bits to garnish.

TIP
Cold roast chicken, pork or beef can be used in this salad.

SHREDDED SPROUT SALAD

SERVES 1

PREP TIME: 10 MINS

WF · GF

2 handfuls **kale**, destemmed and finely shredded

100g (3½oz) **Brussels sprouts**, finely shredded

juice of ½ a **lemon**

3 tablespoons **Leon honey & mustard dressing** (see page 218)

1 tablespoon **dried cranberries**

50g (1¾oz) **cooked bacon lardons** (optional)

25g (1oz) **smoked almonds**, roughly chopped

1 tablespoon finely grated **pecorino**

salt and **freshly ground black pepper**

This is terrifically easily assembled al-desko. The vegetables don't need cooking, and you can add pre-cooked bacon or do it the night before. Keep a sharp knife in your desk, you never know when you might need it.

Place the shredded veg in a bowl and sprinkle with lemon juice. Season well.

Toss with the dressing, along with the cranberries, bacon lardons and almonds.

Fold in the pecorino just before serving.

FARRO & WIDE

SERVES 1
PREP TIME: 15 MINS · COOK TIME: 30 MINS
DF · V · Ve

1 **leek**, cut into 2–3cm (¾–1¼ inch) slices

6 **radishes**, cut in half

1 **fennel bulb**, cut into 8 wedges

1 **turnip**, peeled and cut into wedges

2 tablespoons **olive oil**

½ a clove of **garlic**, crushed

150g (3½oz) **cooked farro**

juice of ½ a **lemon**

salt and **freshly ground black pepper**

GREMOLATA:

1 tablespoon finely chopped **fresh flat- leaf parsley**

grated zest of ½ a **lemon**

½ a clove of **garlic**, very finely chopped

The salad you have been searching for.

Heat the oven to 170°C/325°F/Gas Mark 3.

Toss the prepped vegetables in a tablespoon of the olive oil and roast in the oven for 30 minutes, or until just cooked. Remove from the oven and leave to cool.

While the veg are cooking, heat the remaining oil in a pan, add the garlic and cook for a minute. Tip in the farro and mix with the garlic oil. Cook for a few minutes. Season well, then stir in the lemon juice and leave to cool.

Mix together the ingredients for the gremolata and season to taste. Combine the veg and farro. Sprinkle with the gremolata and fold through the salad.

> ### \\\ TIP ///
> Another easy salad with cooked farro is made by adding chopped tomatoes, piquillo peppers and cooked courgette pieces. Stir through pesto and olive oil.

SPINACH, CHICKPEA & ALMOND

SERVES 1
PREP TIME: 10 MINS · COOK TIME: 1 MIN
WF · GF · DF · V · Ve

1 tablespoon **sultanas**

300g (10½oz) **spinach**

a pinch of **cayenne pepper**

100g (3½oz) **cooked chickpeas**

2 tablespoons **flaked almonds**, toasted

2 tablespoons **marinated red onions**
   (see page 218)

½ a clove of **garlic**, crushed

2 tablespoons **olive oil**

1 tablespoon chopped **fresh
   flat-leaf parsley**

salt

An end-of-the-month strapped-for-cash dish. Tastes so good it will distract you from the shoes you thought you could afford.

Cover the sultanas with hot water and leave to soak.

Cook the spinach in boiling water for a minute, then refresh with cold water and drain well. Squeeze out any excess moisture from the spinach and chop finely, then season with salt and cayenne pepper.

Crush half the chickpeas roughly. Mix all the ingredients together at the last minute, including the drained sultanas.

BEETROOT, LABNEH & DUKKAH

SERVES 1
PREP TIME: 10 MINS
WF · GF · V

200g (7oz) **beetroot**, roasted and cut into chunks

100g (3½oz) cooked **Puy lentils**

4 tablespoons **marinated red onions** (see page 218)

2 tablespoons **olive oil**

1 tablespoon **balsamic vinegar**

a small bunch of **watercress**

2 **radishes**, sliced (optional)

50g (1¾oz) **labneh**

1 tablespoon chopped **fresh mint**

2 teaspoons **dukkah**

salt and **freshly ground black pepper**

Lightly salted labneh adds a creamy subtle richness to this dish and complements the beetroot so much that it blushes pink.

Mix the beetroot chunks with the lentils and red onions. Stir through the olive oil and balsamic, and season well.

Arrange the watercress on a plate and top with the beetroot. Finish with the radish, labneh, mint and dukkah.

FOOD FOR FRIENDS

HEARTY CHOKES & TRUFFLE

SERVES 4
PREP TIME: 10 MINS
WF · GF

8 **Jerusalem artichokes**

2 tablespoons **lemon juice**

50g (1¾oz) **dandelion leaves** (if they're in season) or **frisée**

leaves of 3 **chicory** heads

50g (1¾oz) **Parmesan shavings**

200g (7oz) **polenta croutons** (see page 214)

2 tablespoons chopped **fresh chives**

truffle oil, to serve

DRESSING:

2 tablespoons **lemon juice**

3 tablespoons **extra virgin olive oil**

salt and **freshly ground black pepper**

The dandelion leaves provide a bitter flavour. This is a good thing, rather than a warning. They are tricky to source sometimes, unless you have a garden in need of weeding.

Peel the Jerusalem artichokes, place them in a container and cover them with cold water. Add the lemon juice to stop them discolouring.

Mix together the dressing ingredients and season well.

Toss the dandelion and chicory leaves together in a large bowl. Just before serving, thinly slice the artichokes into the salad using a mandolin or peeler.

Cover with Parmesan shavings, croutons and chives, and drizzle with truffle oil.

\\\ TIP ///

You can add shredded raw Brussels sprouts and crumbled (or grilled) goat's cheese to this salad.

CHEESE & WINTER LEAVES

SERVES 4
PREP TIME: 10 MINS · COOK TIME: 50 MINS
WF · GF

400g (14oz) **squash**, cut into chunks
   or slices
3 tablespoons **olive oil**, plus a little for
   the squash
75g (2¾oz) **pecans**
a dash of **Tabasco**
a dash of **Worcestershire sauce**
a pinch of **cayenne pepper**
200g (7oz) **mixed winter leaves (purslane,**
   radicchio or **frisée)**
2 **ripe pears**, peeled and sliced
1 tablespoon **cider vinegar**
blue cheese dressing (see page 218)
salt and **freshly ground black pepper**

The pears and pecans add a satisfying crunch to this salad, and the blue cheese dressing complements their flavours nicely. The squash base makes it a filler as well as a thriller.

Heat the oven to 200°C/400°F/Gas Mark 6.

Toss the prepped squash in olive oil and season well, then roast in the oven for about 40 minutes, or until tender. Remove and set aside to cool.

Mix the pecans with the Tabasco, Worcestershire sauce, cayenne and some salt. Put on a baking tray and place in the oven for 8 minutes, or until lightly toasted.

To serve, toss the leaves and pears with the olive oil and vinegar and season. Layer with the squash and pecans and drizzle with the blue cheese dressing.

\\\\ **TIP** ////
Add shredded ham hock if
you want to pork it up a bit.

THE HAS-BEAN

SERVES 4
PREP TIME: 10 MINS · COOK TIME: 5 MINS
WF · GF · DF · V · Ve

200g (7oz) **peas**
200g (7oz) **broad beans**
200g (7oz) **sugar snaps**, sliced
3 tablespoons **olive oil**
1 tablespoon **red wine vinegar**
2 cloves of **garlic**, crushed
4 cooked **artichoke hearts**, sliced
100g (3½oz) **Puy lentils**, cooked
3 tablespoons chopped **fresh mint**
200g (7oz) **baby spinach leaves**
a handful of **pea shoots**
salt and **freshly ground black pepper**

This salad has a great legume volume, so it's full of protein. It's fine to use frozen broad beans and peas, and you can find cooked artichokes in most supermarkets and delis.

Blanch the peas, broad beans and sugar snaps in boiling salted water for a couple of minutes.

Whisk together the oil, vinegar and garlic in a large bowl. Drain the peas and beans well and put them into the dressing while still hot, along with the artichokes and lentils. Season well. Stir and leave to cool.

Add the mint to the salad when it has cooled down. Scatter the baby spinach on a serving plate, top with the pea, bean, artichoke and lentil mixture and serve topped with pea shoots.

\\\\ TIP ////

If you fancy making this a bit meatier, you can fold in shredded prosciutto or salami.

SALPICON SEAFOOD

SERVES 4
PREP TIME: 30 MINS
WF · GF · DF

250g (9oz) **cooked mussel meat**
250g (9oz) **cooked king prawns**, peeled
100g (3½oz) **white crabmeat**
1 **courgette**
½ a **cucumber**
½ a **mooli**
1 **carrot**
salt and **freshly ground black pepper**

DRESSING:
½ a **red pepper**, deseeded and
   finely diced
½ a **yellow** or **orange pepper**, deseeded
   and finely diced
½ an **avocado**, finely diced
2 **shallots**, finely chopped
1 clove of **garlic**, crushed
1 **red chilli**, chopped
1 tablespoon **rice wine vinegar**
1 tablespoon **lime juice**
2 tablespoons **rapeseed oil**
1 teaspoon **maple syrup**
1 tablespoon chopped **fresh coriander**
1 tablespoon chopped **fresh chives**

A recipe to take with you on a trip to the seaside.

Fold the seafood together in a large bowl.

Mix together the dressing ingredients, whisking well to combine. Pour the dressing over the seafood and fold through. Place, covered, in the fridge until you are ready to serve.

Peel the courgette, cucumber, mooli and carrot and use a Y-shaped peeler to shave ribbons from each. Toss together and season with salt and pepper.

To serve, top the lettuce and vegetables with the marinated seafood.

\\\\ TIP ////

This can also be made with fresh mussels in the shell – if you do this, reduce the mussel-cooking liquid and add it to the dressing for extra flavour.

GET FIGGY WITH IT

150g (5½oz) **farro**

3 tablespoons **olive oil**

1 large head of **radicchio**

1 tablespoon **balsamic vinegar**

1 clove of **garlic**, crushed

a pinch of **brown sugar**

1 tablespoon chopped **fresh marjoram**

125g (4½oz) **mixed salad leaves**

4 **figs**, quartered

seeds of ½ a **pomegranate**

100g (3½oz) **blue cheese**, crumbled

a handful of **chervil**, to garnish (optional)

salt and **freshly ground black pepper**

One for the onset of autumn. Deep, ripe reds that remind us of the falling leaves, and of trying to work out if it really is true that your conker is stronger if baked.

Rinse the farro and place it in a pan with about 500ml (18fl oz) of water. Add a pinch of salt and bring to the boil. Simmer for about 25 minutes, or until the farro is cooked but still chewy. Drain well, season and stir through 1 tablespoon of olive oil.

Cut the radicchio into thin wedges. While you're doing this, start to heat up the griddle pan. In a large bowl, whisk the remaining 2 tablespoons of olive oil with the vinegar, garlic, sugar and marjoram.

When the griddle is hot, start to grill the radicchio wedges. This can be done in batches – the aim is for the radicchio to wilt and brown slightly. As it comes off the griddle, place it straight into the dressing and toss it around, seasoning as you go.

To assemble the salad, arrange the wilted radicchio on a serving plate with the salad leaves. Sprinkle with the farro and pour over any dressing left over from the radicchio. Finally, top the salad with the figs, pomegranate seeds and crumbled blue cheese, and with the chervil, if liked.

＼＼＼ TIP ／／／

To remove the seeds from a pomegranate, place one half cut side down in the palm of one hand (over a bowl). With the other hand, whack the pomegranate with a rolling pin or heavy object. Seeds should fall out without too much pith.

COD'S ARTICHOKES

SERVES 4
PREP TIME: 30 MINS · COOK TIME: 15 MINS
WF · GF

500g (1lb 2oz) **salt cod**, soaked in water for 24 hours

about 400ml (14fl oz) **milk**

4 tablespoons **olive oil**, plus extra for the fish

200g (7oz) **Jerusalem artichokes**

2 tablespoons **lemon juice**, plus extra for the artichokes

2 large **globe artichokes**

200g (7oz) **chestnut mushrooms**, thinly sliced

125g (4½oz) **baby salad leaves**

salt and **freshly ground black pepper**

truffle oil, to serve

a small bunch of **fresh flat-leaf parsley**, to serve

\\\ TIP ///

To salt cod at home, use very fresh fish and dry well. Cover with salt and leave in the fridge for 48 hours. For this recipe you could also use lightly salted cooked fresh white fish.

Fresh globe artichokes are sometimes difficult to come by and are quite hard to prepare. It is fine to substitute the finely sliced cooked artichokes that can be found at most delis. If cod did fast food.

Rinse the salt cod and remove all skin and bones. Place in a pan and cover with the milk. Poach gently over a low heat until the cod is just cooked. This should take about 15 minutes, but it depends on the quality of the salt cod used. Remove it from the pan when it's done and drain on kitchen paper. Then break the fish into large flakes and toss in a little olive oil.

Peel the Jerusalem artichokes and leave them whole in some water with a little lemon juice. Prepare the globe artichokes by peeling back the outer leaves and cutting back until you get to the heart. Remove the hairy choke with a teaspoon and place the heart in the water with the Jerusalem artichokes.

Finely slice the artichokes either by hand, with a sharp knife, or on a mandolin. Put the mushrooms and salad leaves into a large bowl and fold in the artichokes, then season well and dress with the lemon juice and olive oil.

Arrange on a large serving plate and dot with the flakes of salt cod. Finish with a drizzle of truffle oil and some parsley leaves.

BROC ON SALMON

SERVES 4

PREP TIME: 15 MINS · COOK TIME: 40 MINS

WF · GF

500–600g (1lb 2oz–1lb 5oz) **salmon fillet**, skinned and pin-boned

1 tablespoon **olive oil**

1 tablespoon chopped **fresh rosemary**

250g (9oz) **purple sprouting broccoli**, trimmed

leaves of 2 heads of **chicory**

100g (3½oz) **rocket**

salt and **freshly ground black pepper**

ANCHOVY SAUCE:

8 cloves of **garlic**, peeled

100ml **milk**

5 **anchovy fillets**

50g (1¾oz) **soft butter**

2 tablespoons **olive oil**, plus extra for salmon

If you're not a fan of anchovies, any other garlic-based dressing will work well.

Make the sauce by cooking the garlic in the milk for about 30 minutes, or until soft. If the pan starts to catch, add a little more milk. When it's soft, place the pan contents in a food processor with the anchovies and butter. Blitz, drizzling in the olive oil, until you have a thick dressing.

Rub the salmon with oil and season with lots of salt and pepper. Heat up a griddle pan or grill until it's very hot and place the salmon on it, sprinkling it with rosemary. Cook for 2 minutes on one side, then turn over and repeat. It's good to have the salmon a little pink in the middle – the exact cooking time will depend on the thickness of the fish. Remove from the grill and leave to cool.

Cook the broccoli in boiling salted water for 2 minutes, or until tender. Drain and refresh under cold running water.

Arrange the chicory, rocket and broccoli on plates and season well. Break the salmon into large flakes over the top and drizzle over the anchovy sauce.

\\\\\ **TIP** /////

The anchovy sauce makes a great dip for crudités.

WINTER VEGETABLE SALAD

SERVES 4
PREP TIME: 25 MINS · COOK TIME: 40 MINS
WF · GF · V

1.2kg (2lb 12oz) **mixed winter vegetables**

2 tablespoons **olive oil**

chermoulah dressing (see page 219)

100g (3½oz) **watercress**

100g (3½oz) **labneh**

4 tablespoons **Leon toasted seeds** (see page 215)

1 tablespoon chopped **fresh mint** and **coriander**

salt and **freshly ground black pepper**

The vegetables in this salad can be a mix of any winter ones you like, such as parsnips, carrots, turnips and squash. If you're using beetroots, make sure you cut them into smaller pieces than the others, as they take longer to cook.

Heat the oven to 170°C/325°F/Gas Mark 3.

Peel all the vegetables and cut them into chunks or slices. Toss in a little olive oil and season well. Roast for about 40 minutes, or until the vegetables are tender.

While the vegetables are cooking, make your dressing and put it into a large bowl.

When the vegetables are cooked, and while they're still hot, tip them into the bowl of dressing. Stir to combine, then leave to cool.

Fold together the cold vegetables and the watercress, top with a spoon of labneh, and sprinkle with the seeds and herbs.

＼＼＼ TIP ／／／

To make your own labneh, stir a good pinch of salt into some full-fat yoghurt. Place in a muslin-lined colander sitting over a bowl and leave overnight in the fridge.

FRUITY ROAST CHICKEN

SERVES 4
PREP TIME: 20 MINS · COOK TIME: 10 MINS
DF

2 tablespoons **raisins**

2 tablespoons good **white wine vinegar**, e.g. Moscatel

4 tablespoons **olive oil**

1 clove of **garlic**, crushed

1 tablespoon chopped **fresh chives** and **tarragon**

½ a loaf (about 300g) of **stale ciabatta**

½ a whole **roast chicken**, juices reserved

a bunch of **spring onions** or 2 **shallots**, chopped

3 tablespoons **pine nuts**, toasted

200g (7oz) **white grapes**, halved

150g (5½oz) **rocket**

salt and **freshly ground black pepper**

Using both grapes and raisins is like reconnecting grandparents and grandchildren. A jolly reunion. This recipe is based on the classic salad from Zuni Café in San Francisco.

Heat the oven to 200°C/400°F/Gas Mark 6.

Cover the raisins with very hot water and leave to soak. Mix together the white wine vinegar, olive oil, garlic and chopped herbs to make the dressing and season well.

Rip up the stale bread into 2–3cm (¾–1¼ inch) chunks. Place on a roasting tray and bake in the oven for 5–10 minutes until the bread is lightly browned and crisp. Remove from the oven and tip into a bowl with half the dressing and the roast chicken juices.

Drain the raisins and add them to the bowl. Mix in the spring onions or shallots and pine nuts.

Tear the meat from the chicken, or chop it roughly. Toss with the grapes, rocket and the remaining dressing. Fold into the bread salad and serve immediately.

\ \ \ \ **TIP** / / / /
Chive flowers can be used here to make a lovely garnish.

CRISP-Y DUCK

SERVES 4
PREP TIME: 20 MINS · COOK TIME: 35 MINS
WF · GF · DF

½ teaspoon **five-spice powder**

2 large **duck breasts**

1 **sweet potato**, peeled

2 tablespoons **olive oil**

4 **cooked beetroots**, peeled and cut into wedges

150g (5½oz) **frisée**

1 **orange**, preferably blood, segmented

4 **radishes**, sliced

salt and **freshly ground black pepper**

DRESSING:

1 tablespoon **marmalade**

2 tablespoons **orange juice**

1 tablespoon **rice wine vinegar**

1 teaspoon finely grated **ginger**

2 tablespoons **olive oil**

\\\\ TIP ////

TO COOK THE BEETROOT:
Trim, wash and place on a baking tray with a good drizzle of olive oil and 50ml (1¾fl oz) of water. Season and bake, covered with foil, at 180°C/350°F/Gas Mark 4 for about 1 hour. Once cooked, the skins should come away easily.

The sweet potato crisps are extremely moreish. You may want to make double the prescribed amount for 'tasting' as you go.

Rub the five-spice powder into the skin and flesh of the duck breasts and place them skin side down in a cold frying pan. Turn on the heat and cook the duck for 6 minutes on one side to release the fat and to crisp and brown the breast. Tip out the fat, turn the duck over and cook for another 5 minutes over a medium heat. Remove from the pan and leave to rest for 10 minutes.

While the duck is cooking, heat the oven to 200°C/400°F/Gas Mark 6. Prepare the sweet potato by cutting it into long strips with a peeler or spiralizer. Toss them in the olive oil and season with salt and pepper. Place on a baking tray and cook in the oven for about 20 minutes, turning over occasionally so that the strips are evenly browned and crisp. Remove and tip on to kitchen paper.

Whisk together the dressing ingredients and check the seasoning. Toss the beetroot with a little of the dressing and season.

Dress the frisée and arrange on a serving plate. Slice the duck diagonally and arrange over the salad with the beetroot, orange segments and radishes. Top with the crisp sweet potato.

ASPARAGUS, POTATO & CRAB

SERVES 4

PREP TIME: 15 MINS · COOK TIME: 5 MINS

WF · GF · DF

250g (9oz) **asparagus spears**, trimmed

200g (7oz) **new potatoes**, boiled

1 tablespoon **olive oil**

250g (9oz) **white crabmeat**

100g (3½oz) **mixed salad leaves**

salt and **freshly ground black pepper**

EGG VINAIGRETTE:

2 **eggs**

2 **shallots**, chopped

1 tablespoon chopped **fresh tarragon**

1 tablespoon chopped **fresh flat-leaf parsley**

1 tablespoon chopped **fresh chives** and **chervil**

50ml (2fl oz) **rapeseed oil**

50ml (2fl oz) **light olive oil**

lemon juice, to taste

This dressing method is almost foolproof and the emulsion shouldn't split if you boil the eggs for a few minutes (see mayonnaise method, page 218).

Blanch the asparagus for a few minutes until tender. Drain and season well. Slice the potatoes, then toss in olive oil and season with salt and pepper.

To make the dressing, start by boiling the eggs for 3 minutes. Quickly break the runny yolk into a food processor, add the shallots and herbs, and blitz them all together. Don't throw away the cooked egg whites. Slowly pour in the two oils to make an emulsion, season and add lemon juice to taste. Chop the cooked egg whites finely and stir into the dressing.

Arrange the asparagus on a serving plate with the potatoes, salad and crab, and drizzle with some of the dressing, leaving the rest on the side.

TIP

The dressing is also good with dressed lobster or grilled leeks.

NUTTY CLEMENTINE

SERVES 4
PREP TIME: 15 MINS
WF · GF · V

seeds of 1 **pomegranate**

2 **clementines**, peeled and cut into pieces

50g (1¾oz) **toasted walnuts** (see page 214)

1 **avocado**, sliced

100g (3½oz) **rocket**

leaves from 1 head of **red chicory**

150g (5½oz) **ricotta**

3 tablespoons **Middle Eastern dressing**
  (see page 216)

salt and **freshly ground black pepper**

This salad is loaded with different flavours and textures, and is pretty much guaranteed to make you look like a salad genius to anyone you show it off to. Which is exactly why we've put it in this book for everyone to see.

Place all the salad ingredients, except the ricotta, in a large bowl and season well. Whisk the dressing and toss with the salad.

Place on a serving plate, and top with nuggets of ricotta before serving.

\\\\ TIP ////

It helps to sing 'Oh my darling, Clementine' while you prepare this salad. Or you could replace clementines with satsumas or tangerines and make up your own song. We prefer the Dolly Parton version.

THAI SQUID SALAD

SERVES 4
PREP TIME: 20 MINS · COOK TIME: 10 MINS
WF · GF · DF

1 tablespoon **tamarind paste**

2 tablespoons **fish sauce**

2 tablespoons **palm sugar**

1 clove of **garlic**, crushed

1 **red chilli**, chopped

600g (1lb 5oz) **squid tubes**

3 tablespoons **sunflower oil**

a pinch of **cayenne pepper**

2 **eggs**, beaten

1 tablespoon **rice vinegar**

a pinch of **sugar**

2 **carrots**, cut into fine batons

½ **cucumber**, cut into batons

100g (3½oz) **beansprouts**

a bunch of **spring onions**, chopped

a bunch of **fresh chives**, cut into 3cm
(1¼ inch) lengths

3 tablespoons chopped **fresh coriander**

70g (2½oz) roasted **peanuts**, chopped

2 **limes**, quartered, to serve

The squid become noodles and provide a very good base for this take on a classic pad Thai.

Make the dressing by mixing the first 5 ingredients together until the sugar has dissolved.

Open up the squid tubes and cut them into fine strips or 'noodles'. Heat the oil in a large pan or wok and stir-fry the squid in batches, stirring quickly so that it's just cooked. Season with cayenne pepper.

Add the squid to the dressing and leave to cool.

Beat the eggs with the vinegar and a pinch of sugar. Pour the mixture into a pan, swirl around and cook until it's just set. Remove and slice into strips.

In a large bowl, mix all the remaining vegetables and herbs. Fold in the squid and dressing, top with the peanuts and serve with lime quarters on the side.

> ### \\\\ TIP ////
> Make this salad veggie with mooli strips instead of squid, no fish sauce and extra tamarind in the dressing.

AND THE BEET GOES ON

SERVES 4
PREP TIME: 15 MINS
WF · GF · V

300g (10½oz) **beetroot**, peeled

5 **carrots**, peeled

1 small **mooli**

6 **radishes**

100g (3½oz) **watercress**

2 **oranges**, segmented

70g (2½oz) **feta**, crumbled

2 tablespoons chopped **fresh mint**

1 tablespoon chopped **fresh dill**

DRESSING:

100g (3½oz) **pistachios**, chopped

grated zest and juice of 1 **orange**

1 **red chilli**, chopped

1 clove of **garlic**, crushed

2 tablespoons **marinated red onions**
   (see page 218)

3 tablespoons **olive oil**

1 teaspoon **balsamic vinegar**

salt and **freshly ground black pepper**

Slicing the vegetables thinly allows them to soak up all the fresh zingy dressing. It will make your tastebuds sing.

Prepare all the vegetables by shaving or thinly slicing them. The carrots and mooli can be shaved using a vegetable peeler. The beetroot can too, though it may be easier to slice it. The radishes can be thinly sliced across.

Mix together all the dressing ingredients and toss with the vegetables. Season well.

Put the watercress on a serving plate and arrange the vegetables on top. Finish with the orange pieces, feta and herbs.

\\\\ TIP ////

The dressing can also be used to dress roasted beets and carrots or squash.

COCONUT KINILAW

SERVES 4
PREP TIME: 30 MINS (plus marinating)
WF · GF

500g (1lb 2oz) **fresh megrim sole fillets**, skinned

1 **red onion**, very thinly sliced

½ teaspoon **salt**

100ml (3½fl oz) **coconut vinegar**

½ a **red pepper**, finely diced

½ a **yellow pepper**, finely diced

4 **spring onions**, sliced

¼ **cucumber**, peeled and finely diced

1 **red chilli**, finely chopped

50g (1¾oz) **creamed coconut**

120ml **hot milk** or **coconut water**

½ a clove of **garlic**, crushed

1 teaspoon finely grated **ginger**

a pinch of **cayenne pepper**

¼ teaspoon **ground turmeric**

100g (3½oz) **watercress**

1 **ripe mango**, diced

fresh coriander leaves, to serve

TIP

The megrim sole can be substituted with any white fish.

Coconut vinegar is traditionally used in the Philippines to 'cook' fish – although there's no heat involved, the acid in the vinegar has the same effect. If you can't source it, you can use lemon or lime juice instead.

Remove any bones from the fish and slice it into 1cm (½ inch) pieces. Place in a non-reactive bowl (glass or stainless steel) with the onion, salt and vinegar. Stir and leave covered in the fridge for about 30 minutes. If you're using lemon or lime juice instead of coconut vinegar, only leave for about 15 minutes.

While the fish is in the fridge, mix the peppers, spring onions, cucumber and chilli together in a bowl. When the fish has finished 'cooking', drain it and toss with the diced vegetables.

Grate the creamed coconut and blend it with the hot milk or coconut water, garlic, ginger, cayenne pepper and turmeric. Leave to cool.

To serve, arrange the watercress and some of the mango on a serving plate. Pile up the fish and diced vegetables, drizzle with the dressing and sprinkle with the rest of the mango and the coriander leaves.

AUBERGINE KISIR

SERVES 4

PREP TIME: 20 MINS · COOK TIME: 20 MINS

V

250g (9oz) **bulgur wheat**
1 **red onion**, finely chopped
a pinch of **ground cumin**
1 tablespoon **red pepper paste**
1 teaspoon **tomato purée**
½ teaspoon **salt**
2 tablespoons **olive oil**
1 tablespoon **pomegranate molasses**
2 tablespoons **lemon juice**
4 **spring onions**, chopped
4 **tomatoes**, skinned and chopped
½ **cucumber**, peeled, deseeded and
   chopped
2 tablespoons chopped **fresh
   flat-leaf parsley**
1 **aubergine**, sliced
100g (3½oz) **watercress** (optional)
salt and **freshly ground black pepper**

DRESSING:
200ml **plain yoghurt**
2 tablespoons **tahini**
1 clove of **garlic**, crushed
2 tablespoons **lemon juice**
2 tablespoons chopped **fresh mint**

This is traditional Turkish fare, usually served as a side salad or part of a mezze. Makes us think of kissing. Which is never a bad thing when cooking for friends.

Mix the bulgur wheat with the onion, cumin, pepper paste, tomato purée, salt and 1 tablespoon of olive oil. Stir well to combine. Next, pour over 200ml (7fl oz) of boiling water, stir once and cover with clingfilm. Leave for 15 minutes, then fluff it all up. Stir in the pomegranate molasses, lemon juice and chopped vegetables and parsley. Leave to chill.

Heat up a griddle pan. Toss the aubergine slices in the remaining tablespoon of olive oil and grill them for a minute on each side until they're tender. Season well.

Make the dressing by blitzing together the yoghurt, tahini, garlic and lemon juice. Season, then stir in the chopped mint.

Alternate an aubergine slice with a spoonful of the bulgur wheat and a spoonful of dressing on a serving plate to form a tower. Scatter with the watercress and drizzle more dressing all over.

\\\ TIP ///
If not available, red pepper paste can be made by blitzing peeled roasted red peppers with garlic, chilli and olive oil. A teaspoon of harissa could also be used instead of the paste.

MEXICAN SALAD

3 **cobs of sweetcorn**, with husks

1 **red pepper**

1 **orange pepper**

1 tablespoon **olive oil**

200g (7oz) **cooking chorizo**, sliced

2 **corn tortillas**

1 **avocado**, cut into chunks

100g (3½oz) **small tomatoes**, halved

150g (5½oz) **baby salad leaves**

fresh coriander leaves, to garnish

DRESSING:

2 teaspoons **chipotle sauce**

3 tablespoons **olive oil**

2 tablespoons **lime juice**

½ a clove of **garlic**, crushed

a pinch of **ground cumin**

1 tablespoon chopped **fresh coriander**

\\\ TIP ///
Roasted Halloumi crumbs (see page 215) can be sprinkled over with the tortilla strips.

This is the perfect salad for when you have friends and family over for a barbecue. And for when you don't.

Soak the corn, in its husks, in water for 10 minutes. Drain, then still in the husks, cook on a preheated barbecue or griddle pan for 15 minutes, or until the corn kernels are tender. Leave to cool, then cut the corn kernels away from the cobs in long strips.

Halve the peppers and deseed them. Cut them in half and cook on the barbecue or griddle for a few minutes in half the olive oil, until lightly browned. Slice the peppers into strips.

Heat the oven to 170°C/325°F/Gas Mark 3.

Cook the chorizo slices in a frying pan in the remaining olive oil over a medium heat until lightly browned. Cut the tortillas into strips and toast them in the oven for 10 minutes until golden and crisp.

Whisk together all the dressing ingredients and season.

In a large bowl, toss the corn with the chorizo, peppers, avocado and tomatoes. Coat with the dressing, then on a large serving plate fold them with the salad leaves. Top with the tortilla strips and garnish with extra coriander leaves.

RED CABBAGE WITH BACON & GOATS' CHEESE

SERVES 4
PREP TIME: 15 MINS · COOK TIME: 25 MINS
WF · GF

100g (3½oz) **smoked streaky bacon**, cut into 1–2cm (½–¾ inch) pieces

1 tablespoon **olive oil**

2 **red onions**, sliced

2 tablespoons **balsamic vinegar**

2 teaspoons **soft brown sugar**

½ **red cabbage**, shredded

2 **apples**, cored and diced

50g (1¾oz) **toasted hazelnuts**, roughly chopped

2 tablespoons chopped **fresh flat-leaf parsley**

100g (3½oz) **goat's cheese**, crumbled

salt and **freshly ground black pepper**

This salad is for when it's beginning to look a lot like Christmas. Party season fuel. A good salad to serve both warm and at room temperature.

In a large pan, fry the bacon pieces in the olive oil until lightly browned. Remove with a slotted spoon and drain on kitchen paper.

Tip the onions into the pan along with the balsamic vinegar, sugar and a good pinch of salt. Stir-fry for a few minutes, until the onions have softened. Add the cabbage and cook, stirring, for about 10 minutes until the cabbage wilts.

Season well and continue cooking for another 5 minutes. Remove the pan from the heat and leave to cool until tepid. Add the rest of the ingredients along with the cooked bacon, and serve.

> ＼＼＼ **TIP** ／／／
> Walnuts and feta can be used instead of hazelnuts and goat's cheese.

LAMB SNAP SALAD

SERVES 4

PREP TIME: 20 MINS (plus marinating) · COOK TIME: 10 MINS

WF · GF · DF

2 x 200g (7oz) **lamb leg steaks**

3 tablespoons **olive oil**

2 tablespoons **lemon juice**

½ teaspoon **freshly ground black pepper**

100g (3½oz) **baby spinach leaves**

½ a **head of radicchio**, torn

200g (7oz) **sugar snaps**, sliced

150g (5½oz) **fresh broad beans**

SALSA VERDE:

1 clove of **garlic**, crushed

1 tablespoon **capers**, squeezed dry

3 **anchovy fillets**

leaves from a bunch of **fresh flat-leaf parsley**

leaves from 2 sprigs of **fresh mint**

1 teaspoon **Dijon mustard**

1 tablespoon **red wine vinegar**

100ml (3½fl oz) **olive oil**, plus extra to serve

salt and **freshly ground black pepper**

> \\\\\ TIP /////
>
> If you are using leftover roast lamb, toss thin slices with a little of the salsa verde dressing.

This is a great recipe for using up leftover roast lamb. Make it snappy.

Trim the lamb leg steaks and marinate them in the olive oil, lemon juice and black pepper for at least an hour.

Place the spinach leaves and ripped radicchio in a large bowl. Blanch the sugar snaps and broad beans in boiling water until they're tender, then refresh them under cold running water and drain well. Season with salt and pepper and add them to the salad bowl.

Make the salsa verde by blitzing together the garlic, capers, anchovy fillets, parsley and mint in a food processor. Alternatively, you can chop them by hand. Transfer to a bowl and stir in the mustard and vinegar. Gradually add the olive oil until you have a smooth paste, then season well.

Heat a griddle pan. Grill the lamb leg steaks for 2 minutes on each side, or longer if the steaks are thick. Leave them to rest for 5 minutes, then slice them into 1–2cm (½–¾ inch) chunks.

Toss the salad with a little olive oil and arrange it on a serving plate. Coat the lamb pieces with the salsa verde and fold them into the salad.

WASABI STEAK

SERVES 4
PREP TIME: 15 MINS (plus marinating) • **COOK TIME: 5 MINS**
DF

2 tablespoons **mirin**

2 tablespoons **soy sauce**

1 teaspoon **brown sugar**

1 teaspoon **sesame oil**

400g (14oz) **sirloin** or **rump steak**, cut into 1–2cm (½–¾ inch) slices

1 tablespoon **rapeseed oil**

150g (5½oz) **watercress** or **pea shoots**

200g (7oz) **asparagus**, shaved

150g (5½oz) **cooked edamame beans**

a bunch of **spring onions**, cut into strips

1 tablespoon **black sesame seeds**

1 tablespoon **sesame seeds**

DRESSING:

2 teaspoons **wasabi paste**

1 tablespoon **soy sauce**

2 tablespoons **rice vinegar**

1 tablespoon **light olive oil**

1 teaspoon **brown sugar**

A true umami dish. It hits flavour buds your guests won't know they had.

Mix together the mirin, soy sauce, brown sugar and sesame oil to make a marinade. Place the marinade in a resealable bag with the sliced steak and leave to marinate for an hour or overnight.

Whisk together the dressing ingredients.

Heat the rapeseed oil in a large pan or wok until hot, then carefully lift the steak slices out of the marinade, add to the pan and stir-fry quickly for a minute. Remove from the pan and leave to rest for 5 minutes.

Dress the watercress, asparagus and edamame beans with the dressing. Arrange on a serving plate with the steak and top with the spring onions and sesame seeds.

> **\\\ TIP ///**
>
> The asparagus edamame salad would also be a great accompaniment to plain grilled steak, lamb or chicken.

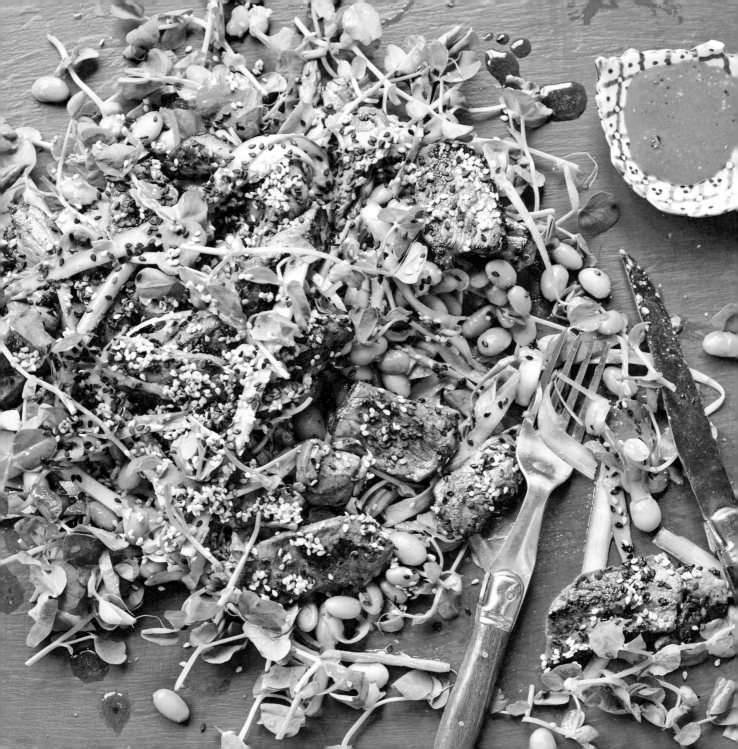

ITALIAN CHICKEN

SERVES 4
PREP TIME: 15 MINS
WF · GF

300g (10½oz) **cooked chicken thighs**, sliced
125g (4½oz) **rocket**
1 **celery heart**, thinly sliced
100g (3½oz) **cooked Puy lentils**
100g (3½oz) **Coppa di Parma slices**, torn
50g (1¾oz) **Grana Padano** slivers
salt and **freshly ground black pepper**

DRESSING:
1 tablespoon **capers**, soaked in cold water, drained and chopped
1 tablespoon **mostarda**, chopped
1 tablespoon **shredded fresh mint**
1 tablespoon **balsamic vinegar**
3 tablespoons **olive oil**

Mostarda is an Italian fruit condiment. If you can't get your hands on it, you can use any dried fruit, for example dried pears.

Whisk together the dressing ingredients.

Toss the chicken with the rocket, celery and lentils and season well, then toss with half the dressing.

Arrange on plates and top with the Coppa di Parma and Grana Padano. Drizzle with the rest of the dressing.

\\\ **TIP** ///
Celery hearts are the tender inner sticks of celery, the first 5cm (2 inches) from the root.

\\\ **TIP** ///

TO COOK PUY LENTILS:
• Rinse well in a colander and drain.
• Place in a pan covered with 3cm/ 1¼ inches of water (or stock).
• Add a few cloves of garlic and sprigs of herbs like sage or rosemary.
• Simmer for about 20 minutes, or until the lentils are just tender.
• Drain and season well while still hot.
• Toss in olive oil.

CHINESE WELLBEING SALAD

SERVES 4
PREP TIME: 20 MINS (plus soaking)
DF · V · Ve

25g (1oz) **arame seaweed**

150g (5½oz) **mooli**, shredded

2 **carrots**, shredded

¼ **cucumber**, deseeded and thinly sliced

100g (3½oz) **shiitake mushrooms**, thinly sliced

1 bunch of **spring onions**, chopped

a handful of **beansprouts**

2 tablespoons **toasted sesame seeds**

mustard cress, to serve

DRESSING:

1 tablespoon **soy sauce**

1 tablespoon **rice vinegar**

1 teaspoon **brown** or **palm sugar**

1 teaspoon **sesame oil**

1 teaspoon grated **ginger**

1 tablespoon chopped **coriander**

This salad cannot move for nutritious goodness. Seaweed and shiitake mushrooms contain so many vitamins and minerals that they've both been used medicinally in East Asia for thousands of years. So, eat well and be well.

Cover the seaweed with plenty of warm water. Leave it for 30 minutes to swell up, then rinse with cold water and drain.

Whisk together the dressing ingredients and prepare all the vegetables.

Mix the vegetables in a large bowl and toss with the dressing. Serve topped with the sesame seeds and mustard cress.

＼＼＼ TIP ／／／
Other dried seaweeds can be used – sea spaghetti has a very good flavour.

FOOD FOR FAMILY

SQUASHED CHILLI, HUMMUS & FETA

SERVES 4
PREP TIME: 15 MINS · COOK TIME: 35 MINS
WF · GF · V

1 **butternut squash**

3 tablespoons **olive oil**

1 tablespoon **cumin seeds**, roasted and ground

2 **red chillies**, sliced

3 cloves of **garlic**, thinly sliced

4 **spring onions**, sliced

2 tablespoons **lemon juice**

50g (1¾oz) **rocket**

100g (3½oz) **hummus**

2 tablespoons **Leon toasted seeds** (see page 215)

salt and **freshly ground black pepper**

DRESSING:

100g (3½oz) **feta**

2 tablespoons **red wine vinegar**

1 tablespoon chopped **fresh mint**

2 tablespoons **olive oil**

This Mediterranean delight is incredibly simple to make and brightens up any mealtime.

Heat the oven to 180°C/350°F/Gas Mark 4.

Cut the squash in half and scoop out the seeds. Cut each half into 4 wedges. Coat with a tablespoon of olive oil and rub with the ground cumin, salt and pepper. Place on a baking tray and cook for 30 minutes, turning halfway through. Leave to cool.

Heat the other 2 tablespoons of olive oil in a frying pan and fry the chillies, garlic and spring onions until the garlic slices just begin to brown. Drain through a sieve, retaining the oil. Mix the oil with the lemon juice and set aside.

Make the feta dressing by crushing the cheese with the vinegar and mint. Stir in the olive oil and let down with about 50ml (2fl oz) of water to the desired consistency. Season with salt and pepper.

Arrange the squash wedges on a serving plate with the rocket. Stir the oil and lemon into the hummus and drizzle over the salad. Sprinkle with the fried chilli, garlic and onion, and the feta dressing. Finish with Leon toasted seeds.

TIP

Top with roasted chickpeas (see page 215) for extra crunch.

PORK BELLY WITH APPLE & WALNUT DRESSING

SERVES 4
PREP TIME: 30 MINS · COOK TIME: 1 HOUR 15 MINS
WF · GF · DF (only **GF** with gluten-free stock)

400g (14oz) **pork belly slices**

200ml (7fl oz) **chicken stock**

1 tablespoon **sunflower oil**

1 tablespoon chopped **fresh rosemary**

2 **fennel bulbs**, trimmed

1 tablespoon **olive oil**

200g (7oz) **cooked French beans**

2 **apples**, cored and diced

200g (7 oz) **purple sprouting broccoli**, trimmed and cooked

4 tablespoons **walnut dressing** (see page 219)

50g (1¾oz) **rocket**

a handful of **toasted walnuts**, to garnish

salt and **freshly ground black pepper**

\ \ \ TIP / / /

Roast pork belly could be used in this salad, cut into small cubes. It is also possible to cook belly pork slices until tender using a contact grill, though care has to be taken because of the amount of fat that comes out of the pork.

Didn't think you could have a Sunday roast salad? Of course you can.

Simmer the pork belly slices in the chicken stock for about an hour until tender. Make sure the pork is covered in stock the whole time – it's fine to top it up with water as you go. Remove the pork, drain it well and pat dry with kitchen paper. Peel away the skin and cut it into 3–4cm (1¼–1½ inch) pieces.

Heat the sunflower oil in a wok until very hot. Add the pork pieces, season well and stir-fry until the pork is crisp. Just before removing the pork from the wok, give it a stir and sprinkle it with the rosemary, then take it out with a slotted spoon.

Finely slice the fennel on a mandolin and toss with the olive oil. Heat a griddle pan and quickly wilt the fennel on the pan in batches. Remove and season.

In a large bowl, mix the fennel with the French beans, apples and purple sprouting broccoli. Add the dressing and fold together.

Arrange the rocket on a serving plate. Top with the dressed vegetables and sprinkle with the pork belly and walnuts.

FREGOLA & CHORIZO

200g (7oz) **cooked fregola**

400g (14oz) **Brussels sprouts**, roasted and halved (see page 190)

½ head of **radicchio**, finely shredded

2 tablespoons **marinated red onions** (see page 218)

1 x 400g (14oz) tin of **borlotti beans**, drained

1 tablespoon **olive oil**, plus extra for drizzling

200g **cooking chorizo**, cut into small cubes

1 tablespoon finely chopped **fresh rosemary**

2 cloves of **garlic**, crushed

1 tablespoon **balsamic vinegar**

30g (1oz) **feta**

2 tablespoons **pine nuts**, toasted

2 tablespoons **fresh flat-leaf parsley** or **chervil leaves**

salt and **freshly ground black pepper**

Fregola is similar to Israeli couscous, but it's a pasta from Sardinia. The bitter radicchio and spicy chorizo make an excellent couple.

In a large bowl, mix the fregola, sprouts, radicchio and onions. Rinse the borlotti beans well, drain and add to the bowl. Season everything well.

Heat the olive oil in a large pan and cook the chorizo until lightly browned. Remove with a slotted spoon and add to the bowl.

Pour away most of the fat in the pan apart from 1 tablespoon. Add the rosemary and garlic to the pan and cook for 1 minute. Pour in the balsamic vinegar and simmer for 1 minute. Remove from the heat and leave to cool until tepid. Pour into the salad bowl and toss everything together.

Arrange in a serving bowl. Finish with a sprinkling of feta, pine nuts and parsley and a drizzle of olive oil.

GRILLED LAMB & GOAT'S CHEESE

SERVES 4
PREP TIME: 20 MINS · COOK TIME: 45 MINS
WF · GF

200g (7oz) small **plum tomatoes**, halved

4 tablespoons **olive oil**

1 clove of **garlic**, crushed

2 tablespoons **fresh oregano**

2 x 200g (7oz) **lamb leg steaks** (grilled as on page 163)

1 **aubergine**, sliced into rounds

a pinch of **ground cumin** and **coriander**

2 teaspoons **balsamic vinegar**

50g (1¾oz) **rocket**

100g (3½oz) **goat's cheese**

2 tablespoons chopped **black olives**

1 tablespoon chopped **fresh mint**

salt and **freshly ground black pepper**

An ideal family supper. It's a crowd-pleaser that will have your dog yapping under the table.

Heat the oven to 120°C/250°F/Gas Mark ½.

Arrange the tomatoes on a baking tray, skin side down. Mix the 3 tablespoons of the olive oil with the crushed garlic. Pound the oregano in a pestle and mortar and add to the oil. Drizzle the oil over the tomatoes and season well. Place in the oven for about 45 minutes, then remove the tomatoes from the tray and set aside. Pour any excess oil or juices into a large bowl.

Leave the lamb to rest, then cut into very thin slices. Heat a griddle until very hot and brush the aubergine slices with the rest of the oil. Grill for a minute on each side, until tender. Remove from the grill and sprinkle with the spices and vinegar.

Toss the aubergine with the tomatoes and rocket, and arrange on a serving plate. Slice the lamb on top of the aubergines and finish by sprinkling with the goat's cheese, olives and mint.

⟍⟍\ TIP /⁄⁄⁄

Sliced leftover roast lamb can be used instead of the grilled lamb leg steaks. The lamb can also be dressed with salsa verde (see page 163).

VERY PERI-PERI CHICKEN

SERVES 4
PREP TIME: 40 MINS (plus marinating) • **COOK TIME: 25 MINS**
WF • GF

2–3 **chicken breasts** or 4–6 **chicken thighs**

1kg (2¼lb) **sweet potatoes**, peeled, sliced and cut into thick batons

2 cloves of **garlic**, finely chopped

1 **red chilli**, chopped

4 **spring onions**, chopped

1 tablespoon **olive oil**

juice of 1 **lime**

70g (2½oz) **baby spinach** or **baby kale leaves**

2 tablespoons chopped **fresh coriander**

1 tablespoon chopped **fresh mint**

½ **yellow pepper**, diced

3–4 tablespoons **ranch dressing** (see page 216)

Leon toasted seeds (optional, see page 215)

salt and **freshly ground black pepper**

MARINADE:

1 clove of **garlic**, crushed

1 tablespoon **lemon juice**

1 tablespoon **red wine vinegar**

1 tablespoon **olive oil**

1 tablespoon **paprika**

a pinch of **cayenne pepper**, to taste

No need to buy peri-peri sauce or seasoning. This version is easy as peri pie. As wild as Friday night.

Mix together the marinade ingredients and rub into the chicken. Leave to marinate for about 2 hours, or preferably overnight.

Heat a griddle pan until hot. Remove the chicken from the marinade and cook for 5 minutes, or until firm to the touch. Turn and cook on the other side for a further 5 minutes, or until firm to the touch. Leave to rest for 10 minutes.

While the chicken is cooking, steam the sweet potato for 15–20 minutes. Tip into a bowl. Cook the garlic, chilli and spring onions in the olive oil for 5 minutes, then fold into the cooked sweet potato with the lime juice. Season well.

Arrange the sweet potato on a large serving plate with the spinach or kale leaves. Slice the chicken and arrange on top. Sprinkle with the herbs and yellow pepper. Drizzle with the ranch dressing.

Top with Leon toasted seeds, if liked.

GADO GADO

200g (7oz) **salad potatoes**, sliced ½cm (¼ inch) thick

150g (5½oz) **firm tofu**, cut into 2cm (¾ inch) dice

rice bran (or other flavourless) **oil**, for deep-frying

200g (7oz) **cabbage**, cooked

100g (3½oz) **beansprouts**

2 **carrots**, cut into thin batons

1 bunch of **spring onions**, cut lengthways

¼ of a **cucumber**, sliced

4 **boiled eggs**, halved

DRESSING:

2 **shallots**, finely chopped

1 clove of **garlic**, crushed

2 **red chillies**, chopped

1 tablespoon **coconut oil**

a pinch of **cayenne pepper**

1 tablespoon **soft brown sugar**

1 teaspoon **tamarind paste**

2 teaspoons *kecap manis*

200ml **coconut milk**

100g roasted **peanuts**, finely ground

1 teaspoon **fish sauce**

juice of ½ a **lime**

This is another salad where any combination of raw and cooked vegetables would work along with the fried tofu and peanut dressing. The name means 'potpourri', but don't eat it in the bathroom.

For the dressing, cook the shallots, garlic and chillies in the coconut oil for 5 minutes until soft. Add the cayenne pepper, sugar, tamarind and *kecap manis*, along with the coconut milk, and bring to the boil. Add the peanuts and 50ml (2fl oz) of water and simmer for 5 minutes. Add the fish sauce and lime juice to taste. The sauce should be the consistency of double cream, so let it cook down to achieve this, if necessary.

Dry the potatoes and tofu with kitchen paper. Heat the oil to about 180°C/350°F, and fry the potatoes and tofu in batches so they are golden and crisp. Drain on kitchen paper.

Arrange the potatoes on a serving plate. Toss the raw and cooked veg with half the dressing. Top with the eggs and tofu. Serve the extra dressing on the side.

\\\\ **TIP** ////
To garnish add *krupuk* (Indonesian prawn crackers), deep-fried.

HARISSA PRAWNS WITH BULGUR

SERVES 4

PREP TIME: 20 MINS · COOK TIME: 10 MINS (plus soaking)

DF

200g (7oz) **bulgur wheat**

400g **raw prawns**, shells removed

1 tablespoon **rose harissa**

4 tablespoons **olive oil**

juice of ½ a **lemon**

200g (7oz) **peas**, cooked

200g (7oz) **sugar snaps**, sliced and cooked

2 tablespoons chopped **fresh dill**

2 tablespoons chopped **fresh mint**

50g (1¾oz) **watercress**

50g (1¾oz) **pea shoots**

handful of **rocket leaves**

salt and **freshly ground black pepper**

Harissa gives a depth and warmth to fish, meat and vegetables that is unrivalled. One of our favourite condiments.

Cover the bulgur wheat with boiling water. Add a good pinch of salt. Cover and leave for about 30 minutes, then fluff up with a fork.

While the bulgur is soaking, coat the prawns with the harissa and season well. Heat a tablespoon of the olive oil in a large frying pan until very hot and quickly fry half the prawns for a minute until they are lightly browned and firm to touch. Remove with a slotted spoon and repeat with the other half.

Whisk together the lemon and the remaining olive oil, and season. Fold the peas and sugar snaps through the bulgur and add half the herbs. Pour over the dressing and fold through the mix.

Transfer to a serving bowl lined with the watercress. Top with the prawns and sprinkle with the rest of the herbs, and the pea shoots and rocket.

GINGER & HONEY SALMON

4 **salmon fillets**, about 100g (3½oz) each

1 tablespoon **sesame oil**

200g (7oz) **black rice noodles** (or
   soba noodles)

50g (1¾oz) **spinach**, cooked and chopped

50g (1¾oz) **samphire**, blanched

½ a **cucumber**, cut into long strips

4 **spring onions**, chopped

1 tablespoon **toasted sesame seeds**

1 tablespoon **black sesame seeds**

fresh coriander leaves

salt and **freshly ground black pepper**

DRESSING:

a 2cm (¾ inch) piece of **ginger**,
   finely grated

1 clove of **garlic**, crushed

juice of 1 **lime**

2 teaspoons **runny honey**

50ml (2fl oz) **sunflower oil**

salt and **cayenne pepper**

Zingy and beautifully interesting to serve. 'Nuff said.

Heat a large griddle pan. Brush the salmon with the sesame oil and season well. Grill for 2 minutes on each side, depending on the thickness of the fillets, until almost cooked through. Remove the salmon from the grill and leave it rest.

Make the dressing by blending all the ingredients together to make an emulsion.

Cook the noodles in lots of salted boiling water for 4–5 minutes and drain well. Refresh with cold water and toss in a large bowl with the spinach, samphire, cucumber and dressing.

To serve, place the salmon on top of the noodles and top with the spring onions, sesame seeds and coriander leaves.

TIP
For knobbly bits of ginger, try using a teaspoon to peel.

INDONESIAN GREENS

SERVES 4
PREP TIME: 20 MINS · COOK TIME: 10 MINS
WF · GF · DF

100g (3½oz) **kale**, de-stalked and shredded

½ a **Chinese cabbage**, shredded

150g (5½oz) **French beans**, trimmed and cut into 1cm (½ inch) lengths

100g (3½oz) **spinach**

100 **beansprouts**

⅓ of a **cucumber**, peeled and cut into 1cm (½ inch) pieces

1 teaspoon *blachan* or **shrimp paste**

1 clove of **garlic**, crushed

2 **shallots**, finely chopped

1 teaspoon **brown sugar**

juice of ½ a **lime**

1 tablespoon **coconut oil**

2 **lime leaves**, shredded (optional)

70g (2½oz) **desiccated coconut**

salt and **cayenne pepper**

The vegetables used here are just an example of what to use in this salad. Carrots, broccoli and cauliflower could also be used and tossed with this fragrant dressing.

Blanch the kale, cabbage, beans and spinach separately (they all take different times to cook). Refresh them in cold water and make sure all excess moisture is squeezed or pressed out of the leaves. Mix in a large bowl with the beansprouts and cucumber.

Crush the next 5 ingredients together to make a paste – either in a pestle and mortar or in a food processor. Heat the coconut oil in a large pan (big enough to hold all the vegetables) and cook the paste for 2 minutes without browning. Add the lime leaves and coconut and stir well to combine. Pour in 150ml (5fl oz) of water and simmer for 5 minutes.

Tip in the vegetables and mix well. Cook for a minute, then tip into a bowl. Check the seasoning and leave the salad to cool to room temperature before enjoying.

\\\ TIP ///

This can be made totally veggie and vegan by using miso paste instead of the shrimp paste.

GET YOUR FREEKEH ON

SERVES 4
PREP TIME: 30 MINS · COOK TIME: 20 MINS

400g (14oz) **Brussels sprouts**

200g (7oz) **Jerusalem artichokes**, peeled

1 teaspoon **maple syrup**

1 tablespoon **olive oil**

150g (5½oz) **cooked freekeh**

2 **red apples**, cored and sliced

100g (3½oz) **medjool dates**, thinly sliced

70g (3½oz) whole **almonds**, toasted and
 roughly chopped

salt and **freshly ground black pepper**

DRESSING

2 teaspoons **date syrup**

1 tablespoon **sherry vinegar**

3 tablespoons **olive oil**

1 **shallot**, finely chopped

1 teaspoon **wholegrain mustard**

TO SERVE:

30g (1oz) **Parmesan cheese slivers**
 (optional)

fresh flat-leaf parsley leaves

If you ever feel like a lady who should lunch, this is the salad for you. Dainty, but punchy.

Heat the oven to 180°C/350°F/Gas Mark 4.

Prepare the sprouts by peeling away any dodgy-looking outer leaves, and cut them into quarters. Slice the Jerusalem artichokes into 1cm (½ inch) thick pieces. Mix them with the sprouts, maple syrup and olive oil. Season well and roast in the oven for about 20 minutes, or until tender. Remove from the oven and leave to cool.

Whisk together all the ingredients for the dressing.

Mix all the salad ingredients with the dressing and arrange on a serving plate. Scatter with the Parmesan slivers and parsley leaves.

TIP
You can use pomegranate molasses instead of date syrup in the dressing.

SMOKED CHICKEN WITH DRIED PEAR

SERVES 4
PREP TIME: 30 MINS
DF

½ a **red pepper**, cut into long strips

½ a **yellow pepper**, cut into long strips

½ a **mooli**, peeled and cut into
thin julienne

1 **carrot**, peeled and cut into thin julienne

1 **small courgette**, cut into thin julienne

2 **smoked chicken breasts**, cut into
long strips

½ a **dried pear**, cut into fine strips

DRESSING:

1 tablespoon chopped **fresh tarragon**

1 tablespoon chopped **fresh mint**

1 **shallot**, finely chopped

1 clove of **garlic**, crushed

1 tablespoon **lemon juice**

2 tablespoons **white wine vinegar**

3 tablespoons **grapeseed oil**

salt and **freshly ground black pepper**

TO GARNISH

fresh mint leaves

a handful of **deep-fried pasta**
(see page 214)

This is based on a recipe from a Texan cookery book that was a gift to Jane from her father in 1987. If you can't find smoked chicken, it is better to have non-smoked than none at all.

Toss together all the vegetables, strips of chicken and pear.

Whisk together the dressing ingredients and pour over the salad. Toss and pile up on a serving plate. Finish with mint leaves and top with deep-fried pasta.

TIP
You could also top this salad with sweet potato crisps (see page 214).

PADSTOW PICNIC

SERVES 4
PREP TIME: 20 MINS

150g (5½oz) **smoked mackerel pâté**
150g (5½oz) **smoked salmon**
100g (3½oz) **dill yoghurt** (see tip below)
a handful of **capers**
200g (7oz) **roasted beetroot**
(see page 144)
150g (5½oz) **rocket**
8 **crispbreads** or **pitta breads**

LEON SLAW:
100g (3½oz) **white cabbage**
100g (3½oz) **red cabbage**
100g (3½oz) **Savoy cabbage**
½ tablespoon chopped **fresh mint**
½ tablespoon chopped **fresh**
flat-leaf parsley
100g (3½oz) **cooked peas**
100ml (3½fl oz) **sesame slaw dressing**
(see page 219)

If you can't get to Padstow, bring it to the park. This is a close cousin of a dish we sometimes serve at Leon. A tribute to the English summer.

To make the slaw, finely shred all the cabbage and roughly chop the herbs. Place in a large bowl, add the peas and dressing and give it a good mix.

Arrange all the ingredients around a central mound of dressed slaw. Keep the salmon, yoghurt and capers together.

＼＼＼ TIP ／／／
To make the dill yoghurt, add chopped fresh dill to Greek yoghurt. Finish with lemon juice to taste and season well.

FOOD FOR FAMILY

ASPARAGUS, MAFTOUL & ORANGE

SERVES 4
PREP TIME: 20 MINS · COOK TIME: 5 MINS
DF · V · Ve

2 bunches of **asparagus**

2 tablespoons **olive oil**

2 **oranges**

1 teaspoon **balsamic vinegar**

2 tablespoons **marinated red onions** (see page 218)

150g (5½oz) **cooked maftoul**

1 **fennel bulb**, shaved

10 large **green olives**, stoned and roughly chopped

2 tablespoons chopped **fresh dill**

4 **radishes**, sliced

salt and **freshly ground black pepper**

Maftoul, Palestinian couscous, is a great ingredient to become familiar with. Boil it like pasta or soak it in boiling water like couscous. A little harder to source than its more common counterparts, but worth the effort.

Trim the asparagus by snapping off the woody ends. Toss in a little olive oil and grill on a preheated griddle pan or in a contact grill (see page 201). Season well, cut into 3cm (1¼ inch) pieces and place to one side.

Finely grate the zest of the oranges into a bowl. Segment the oranges and squeeze the remaining orange flesh (the pithy bit) into the bowl with the zest. Whisk the rest of the olive oil and vinegar into the orange juice. Season with salt and pepper.

Mix the red onions with the maftoul and fennel. Place on a serving dish and top with the asparagus. Scatter with the olives, dill, orange segments and radishes. Drizzle with the orange dressing.

STRAWBERRY, MELON & CHICKEN SALAD WITH ELDERFLOWER

SERVES 4
PREP TIME: 30 MINS
WF · GF

2–3 cooked **chicken breasts**

1 **canteloupe melon**

1 **avocado**

150g (5½oz) **strawberries**

2 **Little Gem lettuces**

2 teaspoons **pink peppercorns**, crushed

1 tablespoon chopped **fresh chives**

DRESSING:

1 tablespoon good **white wine vinegar**

1 teaspoon **elderflower cordial**

1 teaspoon chopped **fresh tarragon**

80ml (5 tablespoons) **grapeseed oil**

50ml (2fl oz) **single cream**

salt and **freshly ground black pepper**

Do you think all berries are told to respect their elderberries? We hope so. This salad is one of our absolute favourites – the elderflower dressing will shock you. In a good way.

To make the dressing, mix all the ingredients together in a liquidizer or by using a stick blender, until you have an emulsion.

Cut the chicken into cubes along with the melon and avocado and place in a bowl. Cut the strawberries in half and add to the bowl, reserving a few for garnish. Coat with the dressing and season.

On a large serving plate, arrange the Little Gem leaves and top with the chicken mix. Finish with a sprinkling of peppercorns, chives and the reserved strawberries.

TIP

If you're prepping this in advance, adding lemon or lime juice will stop your fruit going brown.

GRILLED GREENS

SERVES 4

PREP TIME: 20 MINS · COOK TIME: 5 MINS

DF · V · Ve

400g (14oz) **broccoli**, broken down into small florets (the stalk can be peeled and cut into batons too)

1 tablespoon **olive oil**

200g (14oz) **French beans**, trimmed

200g (14oz) **runner beans**, trimmed and sliced

200g (14oz) **peas**

1 **orange pepper**, thinly sliced

a bunch of **spring onions**, chopped

1–2 **red chillies**, chopped

1 clove of **garlic**, crushed

2 tablespoons chopped **fresh coriander**

leaves from 2 sprigs of **fresh basil**, shredded

1 teaspoon **soy sauce**

juice of ½ a **lime**

salt and **freshly ground black pepper**

A contact grill or griddle is a great piece of kit for cooking vegetables. It's very effective for cooking broccoli quickly – the result is slightly charred and very tasty. If you haven't got access to one, you can blanch your broccoli, then finish it on a hot griddle pan for the same effect. It is also possible to cook the French and runner beans from raw on a contact grill.

Toss the broccoli in olive oil, season and grill on a contact grill for about 3 minutes, or until tender. Blanch the beans and peas until cooked and drain well.

Place the green vegetables in a bowl with the sliced pepper. Mix the rest of the ingredients together and add to the bowl while the vegetables are still warm. Fold together and season well, adding more chilli or lime to taste.

\\\\ TIP ////

To get a smooth garlic paste: finely chop a clove of garlic, then cover with a generous amount of salt and crush with the flat edge of a knife.

SAUSAGE DITALINI

SERVES 4
PREP TIME: 20 MINS · COOK TIME: 20 MINS

300g (10½oz) **cooked sausages**

200g (7oz) **cooked ditalini**

4 **leeks**

1 tablespoon **olive oil**

3–4 tablespoons **Leon honey & mustard dressing** (see page 218)

½ a **cauliflower**, broken into florets and roasted (see page 96)

1 **apple**, cored and thinly sliced

salt and **freshly ground black pepper**

TO GARNISH:

20 **fresh sage leaves**, fried until crisp in **butter**

fresh flat-leaf parsley leaves

Ditalini are so-called because they're diddy and sweet and you can fit a finger through them. This dish, in translation, means sausage fingering. But it's more for forking.

Slice the sausages at an angle, about 1cm (½ inch) thick. Place in a bowl with the cooked pasta.

Slice the leeks in half lengthways and put into boiling salted water for 2 minutes, or until just cooked. Drain well and toss in the olive oil. Heat a griddle pan and grill the leek halves for a minute on each side, until lightly charred. Slice into 1–2cm (½–¾ inch) pieces at an angle, and add to the pasta bowl.

Make the dressing and toss the pasta with the sausages and leeks. Season well. Arrange on a serving plate with the roasted cauliflower, apple and sage leaves. Finish with parsley leaves.

\\\ TIP ///
Bacon or other pork products could be used instead of the sausages, but it would also make a good veggie dish if they were omitted.

BEAN & BACON

8 rashers of **streaky bacon**
1 tablespoon **olive oil**
2 tablespoons **red wine vinegar**
1 teaspoon **wholegrain mustard**
1 tablespoon chopped **fresh chives**, plus
    extra to garnish
2 tablespoons **olive oil**
1 teaspoon **maple syrup**
200g (7oz) **French beans**, trimmed
200g (7oz) **sugar snaps**, trimmed and cut
    in half lengthways
250g (9oz) **haricot** or **cannellini beans**,
    cooked
1 **Romaine lettuce**
2 tablespoons grated **Parmesan**
salt

DRESSING:
2 tablespoons **mayonnaise**
2 tablespoons **soured cream**
1 tablespoon **lemon juice**
2 teaspoons finely chopped **fresh**
    tarragon
1 teaspoon **Dijon mustard**
salt and **freshly ground black pepper**

This combines crisp romaine with a creamy Dijon dressing and a contrasting bean salad. Bacon makes everything better (especially if you buy it nitrate free).

Make the creamy dressing by whisking together all the ingredients.

Slice the bacon into 2cm (¾ inch) pieces. Cook in the olive oil in a large pan until lightly browned and crisp. Remove from the pan with a slotted spoon and drain on kitchen paper.

Transfer 1 tablespoon of bacon fat to a bowl and add the next 5 ingredients. Whisk to combine.

Blanch the beans and sugar snaps in boiling salted water until tender. Drain and toss while hot in the bacon fat dressing with the haricot beans.

Cut the romaine lettuce into quarters. Arrange on a serving plate and drizzle with the creamy dressing. Sprinkle with the Parmesan and extra chives. Pile the dressed beans on the plate and top with the bacon.

PAELLA DELI SALAD

SERVES 4
PREP TIME: 30 MINS (plus soaking) • **COOK TIME: 20 MINS**
WF • GF • DF (check chorizo for dairy products)

a pinch of **saffron**

250g (9oz) **long-grain rice**

1 tablespoon **olive oil**

1 **onion**, finely chopped

1 teaspoon **smoked paprika**

350ml (12fl oz) **gluten-free chicken stock**

100g (3½oz) **cured chorizo salami** (not cooking chorizo), in either thin slices or chunks

100g (3½oz) **artichoke hearts**, sliced

200g (7oz) **prawns**, cooked

150g (5½oz) **peas**, cooked

150g (5½oz) **French beans**, cooked

100g (3½oz) **piquillo pepper strips**

1 **orange**, cut into slices

2 tablespoons chopped **fresh flat-leaf parsley**

fresh flat-leaf parsley leaves, to garnish

salt and **freshly ground black pepper**

DRESSING:

1 teaspoon **sweet paprika**

grated zest of 1 **orange**

1 clove of **garlic**, crushed

1 tablespoon **red wine vinegar**

3 tablespoons **olive oil**

A taste of Spain, at your dinner table. This is one of the longest recipes in this little book, but it is basically an assembly job once the rice is cooked, and it couldn't be more worth it. The ingredients here are just suggestions – you could substitute cooked squid rings, mussels, fish or chickpeas and different vegetables.

Soak the saffron in 50ml (1¾fl oz) of very hot water. Rinse the rice with cold water, then leave it, covered, in water to soak for 30 minutes. Drain well.

Heat the olive oil in a large pan and cook the onion for 5 minutes. Tip in the drained rice with the smoked paprika and cook for a minute, seasoning with salt and pepper and coating the rice with oil. Add the soaked saffron and chicken stock and bring to a simmer. Cover, then allow to cook for about 15 minutes. Leave to stand for 5 minutes before fluffing up with a fork. Tip out of the pan and leave to cool.

While the rice is cooking, whisk together the dressing ingredients and season. Prepare all the other ingredients for the paella.

Layer your ingredients up on a large serving plate, seasoning as you go. Scatter the rice over the plate, then top with the other ingredients, finishing with the orange slices and parsley leaves. Drizzle with the dressing.

\\\\ **TIP** ////
This would also be stunning made with cooked black rice.

ASPARAGUS, PROSCIUTTO & EGG

SERVES 4
PREP TIME: 20 MINS · COOK TIME: 15 MINS
WF · GF · DF

300g (10½oz) **asparagus spears**, trimmed

3 tablespoons **olive oil**

leaves from a sprig of **fresh thyme**

8 slices of **prosciutto**

3 **Little Gem lettuces**

2 teaspoons **balsamic vinegar**

3 **hard-boiled eggs**

30g **Parmesan crisps** (see page 215)

2 tablespoons chopped **fresh chives**

salt and **freshly ground black pepper**

Shaved egg and Parmesan crisps are a revelation.

Heat the oven to 200°C/400°F/Gas Mark 6.

Toss the asparagus with a tablespoon of the olive oil. Season well and place on a baking tray. Sprinkle with thyme leaves and place in the oven for 5–8 minutes, or until the asparagus is just cooked. Remove and leave to cool.

Place the prosciutto slices on baking parchment and pop them into the oven for 5 minutes. They should shrink and become crisp.

Cut the Little Gems into wedges. Mix together the balsamic vinegar and remaining olive oil in a large bowl and season well. Heat a griddle pan and grill the Little Gem wedges until lightly charred and wilted. Toss in the dressing while they're still hot.

Arrange the Little Gems on a large serving plate. Top with the roasted asparagus and crumble over the prosciutto. Grate the egg over the salad and finish with Parmesan crisps and chives.

KOSAMBARI

SERVES 4
PREP TIME: 15 MINS (plus soaking) • **COOK TIME: 5 MINS**
WF • GF • DF • V • Ve

4 tablespoons **moong dhal**, soaked in
    lots of water overnight
3 **carrots**, grated
1 **cucumber**, peeled, deseeded
    and chopped
1 **green mango**, grated
1 tablespoon **coconut oil**
2 teaspoons **mustard seeds**
a pinch of **asafoetida**
10 **curry leaves**
1 teaspoon **ground cumin**
juice of ½ a **lemon**
2 **green chillies**, chopped
fresh coriander leaves
salt and **freshly ground black pepper**

This southern Indian pulse salad is used at celebratory meals. It's so comforting it may as well be a hug from grandma.

Drain the moong dhal well in a sieve and prepare the vegetables and mango.

Heat the coconut oil in a large pan and add the mustard seeds, asafoetida, curry leaves and cumin. Cook, stirring continuously until the mustard seeds start to pop. Add the drained dhal and stir-fry for 3 minutes. Tip into a large bowl and leave to cool.

Add the grated and chopped veg to the bowl. Stir in the rest of the ingredients and season.

\\\ TIP ///

Don't be put off by the smell of asafoetida. It's very strong, but it really livens up the dish. Grated coconut can also be added to this salad.

BKT

250g (9oz) **cherry tomatoes**, halved

3 tablespoons **olive oil**

1 clove of **garlic**, crushed

2 tablespoons **fresh oregano**

200g (7oz) **kale**, de-stemmed and shredded

200g (7oz) **smoked streaky bacon**, cooked and sliced

1 **avocado**, chopped

150g (5½oz) **croutons** (see page 214)

3 tablespoons **ranch dressing** (see page 216)

1 tablespoon chopped **fresh chives**

salt and **freshly ground black pepper**

This is Jane's take on the BLT. A new classic.

Heat the oven to 120°C/250°F/Gas Mark ½.

Arrange the tomatoes on a baking tray, skin side down. Mix the olive oil with the crushed garlic. Pound the oregano in a pestle and mortar and add to the oil. Drizzle the oil over the tomatoes and season well. Place in the oven for about 45 minutes, then remove the tomatoes from the tray and set aside. Pour any excess oil or juices into a large bowl.

Place the shredded kale in the bowl of tomato oil and toss to coat. Season well, then add the bacon, avocado, croutons and roasted tomatoes.

Transfer to a serving plate, drizzle with the ranch dressing and sprinkle over the chives.

\\\\ **TIP** ////

The fresh oregano can be replaced with half the amount of dried oregano.

CRUNCHY THINGS

These are great little add-ons for any simple salad to give a bit more texture, substance and lift.

SOURDOUGH CROUTONS

DF · V · Ve

Toss small pieces of sourdough or other firm-textured bread in a little olive oil and cook on a tray in a heated oven, 180°C/350°F/Gas Mark 4, for about 15 minutes, or until golden brown. Using oil that has been flavoured with garlic gives a good result, and adding whole cloves of garlic to the bread before roasting will give you soft garlic that can be crushed into a dressing.

IKAN BILIS

WF · GF · DF

These are dried small anchovy-like fish that are used in parts of Asia. They can be dry-fried or cooked in a little oil until crisp. They make a great topping for Asian salads and combine well with roasted peanuts.

TOASTED NUTS

WF · GF · DF · V · Ve

It's always best to toast/roast any nuts that you are going to use in salads. Cooking them for 5 minutes in a heated oven, 180°C/350°F/Gas Mark 4, will result in a better flavour, especially if they are sprinkled with salt and spices.

PANGRATTATA

DF · V · Ve

These are basically deep-fried breadcrumbs. The best result comes from frying them in olive oil flavoured with herbs and garlic. Stale bread with crusts removed can be blitzed in a food processor to make the breadcrumbs. Cook a few cloves of garlic and sprig of thyme in the oil until the garlic is golden, then remove from the oil with a slotted spoon and use the oil to fry the breadcrumbs until crisp and golden. Drain well and season. The leftover oil can be used for cooking.

POLENTA CROUTONS

DF · V · Ve

Cooked (or ready-made) polenta, cut into 1–2cm (½–¾ inch) chunks, can be tossed in a little olive oil and baked on a lined tray in a heated oven at 200°C/400°F/Gas Mark 6 for about 20–30 minutes, or until brown and crisp. Alternatively, the chunks can be shallow-fried, but it is best to dust them with a little flour (or cornflour) before frying.

DEEP-FRIED PASTA

DF · V

This is a great use for leftover cooked pasta or fresh egg pasta, especially because of all their interesting shapes and sizes. Deep- or shallow-fry the pasta in rapeseed or sunflower oil until golden and crisp, then drain on kitchen paper.

SWEET POTATO CRISPS

WF · GF · DF · V · Ve

1 **sweet potato**, peeled

2 tablespoons **olive oil**

salt and **freshly ground black pepper**

1. Heat the oven to 180°C/350°F/ Gas Mark 4.
2. Cut the sweet potato into long strips with a peeler or spiralizer. Toss it in the olive oil and season with salt and pepper.
3. Place the sweet potato strips on a baking tray and cook in the oven for about 20 minutes, turning them over occasionally so that the strips are evenly brown and crisp.
4. Remove, tip on to some kitchen paper and season.

LEON TOASTED SEEDS

WF · GF · DF · V · Ve

50% **sunflower seeds**
25% **golden linseeds**
25% **sesame seeds**

1. Toast each type of seed separately by dry-frying them in a pan over a medium heat for 2–3 minutes, or until golden.
2. Mix together for a great topping.

ROASTED CHICKPEAS

WF · GF · DF · V · Ve

2 × 400g (14oz) tins of **chickpeas**, or 500g (1lb 2oz) **cooked chickpeas**
a pinch of **cayenne pepper**
a pinch of **ground cumin**
2 tablespoons **olive oil**
salt and **freshly ground black pepper**

1. Heat the oven to 200°C/400°F/Gas Mark 6.
2. Drain the chickpeas well and rinse in cold water. Dry with a cloth or by rubbing with kitchen paper.
3. Put the chickpeas into a bowl and toss with the spices and olive oil. Place them on a baking tray lined with baking parchment and bake in the oven for about 30 minutes, shaking the tray every 10 minutes to ensure they are cooking evenly.
4. Turn the oven off and leave for 10 minutes.

PARMESAN CRISPS

WF · GF

25g (1oz) roughly grated **Parmesan**
25g (1oz) finely grated **Parmesan**

1. Heat the oven to 200°C/400°F/Gas Mark 6.
2. Line an ovenproof tray with baking parchment. Mix the Parmesan together and pile on to the tray in 2–3cm (¾–1¼ inch) mounds about 4–5cm (1½–2 inches) apart. Bake in the oven for 5–6 minutes.
3. Remove from the tray with a palette knife and place on a wire rack. If the crisps fall apart, don't worry, just sprinkle them on.

ROASTED HALLOUMI CRUMBS

WF · GF · V

250g (9oz) **halloumi**
2 tablespoons **olive oil**
a good grind of **black pepper**
a pinch of **salt**

1. Heat the oven to 220°C/425°F/ Gas Mark 7.
2. Cut the cheese into small 0.5cm/ ¼ inch pieces, or slice and crumble. Toss in the olive oil, then sprinkle over a lined baking tray and season well.
3. Bake in the oven for about 6–8 minutes, or until the halloumi is golden brown.
4. Leave to cool.

DRESSINGS

All the dressings can be whisked together or shaken in a jam jar unless otherwise stated.

OUR FRENCH VINAIGRETTE

WF · GF · DF · V · Ve

1 **sweet potato**, peeled
1 **shallot**, finely chopped
1 teaspoon **Dijon mustard**
1 tablespoon **white wine vinegar**
½ a clove of **garlic**, crushed
2 teaspoons **water**
3 tablespoon **olive oil**
1 teaspoon **maple syrup**

HERB DRESSING

WF · GF · DF · V · Ve

1 clove of **garlic**, crushed
1 tablespoon **white wine vinegar**
1 teaspoon **maple syrup**
3 tablespoons olive oil
2 tablespoons mixed chopped **fresh
     herbs (tarragon, chives , chervil , basil)**

MIDDLE EASTERN DRESSING

WF · GF · DF · V · Ve

3 tablespoons **olive oil**
1 tablespoon **pomegranate molasses**
1 tablespoon **lemon juice**
a pinch of **sumac**
1 tablespoon chopped **fresh dill** and **mint**

LEON TAMARI & SESAME

DF · **V** (can be **WF** and **GF** if you use
gluten-free tamari)

3 tablespoons **sunflower oil**
1 tablespoon **rice vinegar**
1 teaspoon **lemon juice**
1 teaspoon **honey**
1 tablespoon **tamari** (or **soy**)
a dash of **sesame oil**
½ a clove of **garlic**, crushed
3 tablespoon **olive oil**

RANCH DRESSING

WF · GF · V

1 tablespoon **mayonnaise**
1 tablespoon **buttermilk**
1½ tablespoons **soured cream** or
     plain yoghurt
1 tablespoon **cider vinegar**
1 teaspoon **maple syrup**
1 tablespoon **olive oil**
1 tablespoon chopped **fresh chives,
     parsley** and **dill**
½ a clove of **garlic**, crushed
a pinch of **smoked paprika** (optional)
a pinch of **dry mustard powder** (optional)
Tabasco, to taste (optional)

WASABI & SOY

DF · V · Ve

2 teaspoons **wasabi paste**
1 tablespoons **soy sauce**
2 tablespoon **rice vinegar**
1 tablespoon **light olive oil**
2 teaspoons **soft brown sugar**

BASIL DRESSING

WF · GF · DF · V · Ve

½ a clove of **garlic**, crushed
leaves from a small bunch of **fresh basil**
2 tablespoons **olive oil**
salt and **freshly ground black pepper**

Blitz together in a food process or crush
together in a pestle and mortar.

CORIANDER, CHILLI & LIME

WF · GF · DF · V · Ve

3 tablespoons **olive oil**
juice of ½ a **lime**
1 **red chilli**, chopped
1 clove of **garlic**, crushed
2 tablespoons chopped **fresh coriander**

DRESSINGS

LEON HONEY & MUSTARD

WF · GF · DF · V

5 tablespoons **olive oil**
2 tablespoon **cider vinegar**
2 teaspoons **honey**
2 teaspoons **grain mustard**
1 teaspoon **Dijon mustard**

MARINATED RED ONIONS

WF · GF · DF · V · Ve

2 **red onions**, finely sliced or chopped
2 teaspoons **soft brown sugar**
1 tablespoon good **red wine** or
   balsamic vinegar
a good pinch of **salt**

1. Toss the onions in the sugar, vinegar and salt.
2. Cover and leave to marinate at room temperature for anything from 20 minutes to a few hours.

CHILLI PARSLEY GARLIC

WF · GF · DF · V · Ve

2 cloves of **garlic**, crushed
2 **red chillies**, chopped
2 tablespoons chopped **fresh parsley**
juice of ½ a **lemon**
3 tablespoons **olive oil**
salt and **freshly ground black pepper**

BLUE CHEESE DRESSING

WF · GF · V

100g (3½oz) **blue cheese**, crumbled
50ml (2fl oz) **soured cream**
50ml (2fl oz) **buttermilk**
1 tablespoon **red wine vinegar**
½ a clove of **garlic**, crushed
1 teaspoon **maple syrup**

1. Beat the blue cheese with the sour cream and buttermilk. Add the rest of the ingredients and season to taste.
2. Add water to thin down the dressing to the desired consistency. Use as a dressing or a dip.

MAYONNAISE

WF · GF · DF · V

1 **egg**
1 teaspoon **Dijon mustard**
100ml (3½fl oz) **rapeseed oil**
100ml (3½fl oz) **olive oil**
lemon juice, to taste

1. Place the egg in boiling water for 2 minutes.
2. Immediately crack the egg into a food processor and scrape any cooked white out the shell. Blitz with the mustard and slowly add both types of oil until you have a thick emulsion.
3. Add lemon juice to taste.

GARLIC MAYONNAISE:
Crush a clove of **garlic** to a smooth paste with a little **salt** and stir into 3 tablespoons of **mayonnaise**.

MUSTARD MAYONNAISE:
Add 1 teaspoon each of **English**, **Dijon** and **wholegrain mustard** to 3 tablespoons **mayonnaise**.

CHERMOULAH

WF · GF · DF · V · Ve

2 teaspoons **cumin seeds**
1 teaspoon **coriander seeds**
1 teaspoon **fennel seeds**
juice of ½ a **lemon**
1 tablespoon **red wine vinegar**
1 clove of **garlic**, crushed
a pinch of **ground cinnamon**
2 teaspoons **smoked paprika**
1 **shallot**, finely chopped
1 teaspoon **soft brown sugar**
1–2 **red chillies**, chopped
3 tablespoons **olive oil**
salt and **freshly ground black pepper**

1. Dry-roast the cumin, coriander and fennel seeds until fragrant, then grind to a powder.
2. Add to the rest of the ingredients. This can be used as a marinade or a dressing.

ITALIAN

WF · GF · DF · V · Ve

1 tablespoon **balsamic** or red wine vinegar, or the **juice of** ½ a **lemon**
3 tablespoons **olive oil**

SESAME SLAW DRESSING

WF · GF · DF · V · Ve

125ml (4fl oz) **sunflower oil**
3½ tablespoons **soya milk**
2 tablespoons **lime juice**
1 teaspoon **Dijon mustard**
½ teaspoon **tahini paste**
2 tablespoons **white wine vinegar**
1½ tablespoons **water**
salt and **freshly ground black pepper**

1. Place the soya milk, lime juice, Dijon mustard and tahini paste in a bowl and mix.
2. Slowly whisk in the oil until it is all emulsified. Then stir in the water and seasoning.

WALNUT DRESSING

WF · GF · DF · V

1 clove of **garlic**, crushed
1 teaspoon **Dijon mustard**
1 teaspoon **runny honey**
2 tablespoons **cider vinegar**
50ml **sunflower** or **rapeseed oil**
1 tablespoon **walnut oil**
2 tablespoons crushed roasted **walnut pieces**

CAESAR DRESSING

WF · GF

1 **egg**
1 clove of **garlic**, crushed
2 teaspoons **Dijon mustard**
5 **anchovy fillets**
a dash of **Worcestershire sauce**
a dash of **Tabasco**
100ml (3½fl oz) **rapeseed oil**
100ml (3½fl oz) **olive oil**
1 tablespoon **white wine vinegar**
2 tablespoons finely grated **Parmesan**
lemon juice, to taste
salt and **freshly ground black pepper**

1. Place the egg in boiling water for 2 minutes.
2. Immediately crack the egg into a food processor and add the garlic, mustard, anchovies and sauces. Blitz for 30 seconds, then pour in the oils slowly to make an emulsion.
3. Stir in the vinegar, Parmesan and lemon juice to taste. Season well.

INDEX

INDEX

AUTHORS

. . . .

JANE BAXTER

Jane Baxter is the co-author of *Leon Fast Vegetarian* with Henry Dimbleby and has a weekly column in the *Guardian*'s *Cook* supplement. She also co-authored *The Riverford Farm Cook Book*, which won Best First Book at the Guild of Food Writers' Awards. Jane worked at the Carved Angel in Dartmouth and the River Cafe London before becoming the Head Chef at the Field Kitchen, the restaurant for Riverford Organic Vegetables. She now spends her time catering, consulting on food matters and hosting food events in unusual locations.

JOHN VINCENT

John Vincent, Leon's Co-founder, wrote the bestselling *Leon Naturally Fast Food* with Henry Dimbleby and *Leon Family & Friends* with Kay Plunkett-Hogge. John co-wrote the Government's School Food Plan, with Leon co-founder Henry Dimbleby, which resulted in practical cooking and nutrition being put on the curriculum for the first time, and free school lunches for all infant children. John likes food, and Jane.

THE MAKING OF THIS BOOK HAS BEEN AS HAPPY AS THE SALADS.

. . . .

The LEON team were a group of first-timers who have worked with us to create a book that is as fresh as the food. In the spirit of Leon, they have had big ideas, little ideas, and have done a ton of doing.

Thank you to Jo Ormiston for maintaining the vision, art directing, sourcing props and designing a beautiful book. Saskia Sidey for being quite brilliant and quietly pulling (and punning) the whole thing together – without anyone realizing (and diplomatically kicking Baxter's backside). Saskia and Jo have shown why I have so much belief in their talents and partnership.

Thanks to Rachael Gough for late night edits and additions, always being on hand to help and making everyone laugh. Tom Davies for sous cheffing and being on call to lift all the heavy props.

We are in photographic awe of Tamin Jones, who has made sure that each salad here speaks a thousand happy words. And been a total peach to work with.

Stephanie Howard assisted Tamin gracefully and kept everything in its happy place, while keeping a happy face.

Victoria Spicer and Liberty Greene Fennel for assisting, propping and chopping.

Angela Dowden for her super speedy and thorough nutritional analysis.

Adam and Sophie Blaker for letting us invade your house, putting up with all the leftovers and Nat for making the best bonfire.

Katie, Eleanor and Natasha for being great hosts.

Marianne Sidey for letting us raid your kitchen and John Lewis for giving us some tools to ease all the slicing.

Jonathan Christie and Alison Starling at Octopus for sorting everything out, lifting us up and making it all happen.

Pauline Bache for incredible editing, cycling off to get tea towels and always having a spare avocado.

And of course, thank you to everyone who works at Leon every day to make it easy for everyone to eat well. We are blessed to work with you.

An Hachette UK Company
www.hachette.co.uk

First published in Great Britain in 2016 by
Conran Octopus Limited, a division of
Octopus Publishing Group Ltd
Carmelite House
50 Victoria Embankment
London EC4Y 0DZ
www.octopusbooks.co.uk

Text copyright © Leon Restaurants Ltd 2016
Design and layout copyright © Conran Octopus Ltd 2016

Distributed in the US by
Hachette Book Group
1290 Avenue of the Americas
4th and 5th Floors
New York, NY 10020

Distributed in Canada by
Canadian Manda Group
664 Annette St.
Toronto, Ontario, Canada M6S 2C8

A CIP catalogue record for this book is available from the British Library.

Photography by Tamin Jones

Publisher: Alison Starling
Senior Editor: Pauline Bache
Art Direction, Styling and Design (for Leon):
Jo Ormiston
Creative Director: Jonathan Christie
Copywriter and Brand Manager (for Leon):
Saskia Sidey
Senior Production Manager: Katherine Hockley

ISBN 978 1 84091 718 5
Printed and bound in China

10 9 8 7 6 5 4 3 2 1